HITLER'S
WILL

HITLER'S WILL

HERMAN ROTHMAN
Edited by Helen Fry

Dedication
This book is dedicated to Herr Belgart,
the police inspector in Berlin who saved my family's life.
A truly 'righteous Gentile'

First published 2009
This paperback edition published 2014

The History Press
The Mill, Brimscombe Port
Stroud, Gloucestershire, GL5 2QG
www.thehistorypress.co.uk

British Library Cataloguing in Publication Data.
A catalogue record for this book is available from the British Library.

ISBN 978 0 7509 6203 2
Printed in Great Britain

Contents

Foreword

by Dr Helen Fry

The title of Herman Rothman's autobiography, *Hitler's Will*, has a double meaning. It tells the story of Herman (Hermi) Rothman, the last surviving German-speaking interrogator in the British Army who was part of the team that found and translated Hitler's political and personal Will, along with Goebbels' addendum. But *Hitler's Will* is also about the great fight of a family for survival against Hitler's will to kill all the Jews, including them. Hermi's interrogation work at the end of the war meant that he discovered and exposed many of the Nazis' darkest secrets including the documentation from Perry Broad, a German corporal, who confessed in detail to how the Auschwitz concentration camp was run. The document created and interrogations done by Hermi, as well as his testimony in court at the Auschwitz Trial in 1964, led to the conviction of several SS concentration camp staff. But Hermi's story goes far deeper than one man's extraordinary work in Germany with British counter-intelligence at the end of the war. It is a Holocaust memoir of a family separated by the Nazi regime, its survival against all odds, and its reunion after fifteen years.

Hermi was born Hermann Rothman in Berlin in 1924. Less than ten years later, Hitler came to power in Germany. Like all German Jews, Hermi's family was at risk. In the coming years their future changed beyond their imagination and eventually the whole family had to flee the Nazis. Hermi himself was one of 10,000 children who came to Britain on the Kindertransport just before war broke out in September 1939. When he was old enough to enlist, he volunteered for the British Army and was part of another 10,000 refugees from Nazism (not all Kindertransport) who served in the British forces during the Second World War. The wider background and story about these veterans has been told in detail in my book *The King's Most Loyal Enemy Aliens: Germans who Fought for Britain in the Second World War.*

While Hermi had escaped with the Kindertransport, back in Germany his father, mother and brother were forced to go on the run from the Nazis. Woven into this heart-rending tale is the selfless dedication of one family friend, Herr Belgart, a non-Jewish Police Inspector in Berlin, without whom the family would not have survived. At every point, he forewarned them of impending danger and arrest. He informed the family of the imminent deportation of Polish Jews from Berlin in October 1938, and a few weeks later, when Hermi's father was sent by the Gestapo to Sachsenhausen concentration camp, Herr Belgart spent eight months trying to get him out and eventually secured his release. He then helped Hermi's father to get out across Germany before the Gestapo had a chance to re-arrest him. Hermi has dedicated his book to Herr Belgart who did not think twice about risking his own life and position to save members of the Rothman family. Without him, they would not have survived the death camps. Sadly, Herr Belgart did not survive the war, but was killed in the Allied bombing of Hamburg in 1943.

The war in Europe officially came to an end on 8 May 1945, VE Day. Hermi had the satisfaction of witnessing the total defeat of the regime that had caused his flight from Germany in 1939 and so much suffering to his family. Germany had accepted unconditional surrender and much of the country lay in ruins. As the Allies were beginning the enormous task of de-Nazifying and rebuilding Germany and Austria, and shaping postwar Europe, Hermi was posted with the 3rd British Counter-Intelligence Section to Westertimke and then Fallingbostel. It was at the German POW camp in Fallingbostel that Hermi's interesting intelligence work began. He and a handful of fellow German-speaking refugees in the British Army were involved in the interrogation of suspected Nazi war criminals, as well as high-ranking Nazis who had been close to Hitler, including Hermann Karnau. It was at Fallingbostel that one of Hermi's colleagues found Hitler's political and personal Will and Goebbels' addendum sewn into the sleeve-lining of the jacket of POW Heinz Lorenz, who was Goebbels' press attaché. That discovery led to Hermi's unit, under Captain Rollo Reid, translating the valuable documents behind closed doors. Coming into close proximity with men suspected of horrendous war crimes was never going to be easy, but returning to Germany in British Army uniform, Hermi was desperate to demonstrate the order of law, to uphold human rights, and show that despite the personal trauma of the Hitler regime, he could be above the lure of revenge. Today, his desire is that we should all learn from history and not repeat the errors of the past. I commend his courage in writing this book, and in so doing confronting some of the most painful parts of his past. I have met frequently with Herman and Shirley and know how deeply the scars remain within. In recording his story for posterity, he has added a vital piece in the jigsaw of Holocaust oral testimony, against those who would deny the Holocaust ever happened or that it was not as horrific as portrayed by Jews today. Hermi is a man of integrity, devoted to his wife and family, whose gentle humility sometimes hides a truly extraordinary person.

Acknowledgements

My brother and I are only too aware of how much we, our extended family and countless others, owe to the courageous figure of Herr Belgart, a truly 'righteous Gentile', to whom I have dedicated this book. Although this book charts part of my life it also refers to his deeds and the effect it had on our lives. Without being over-dramatic, would we have survived without his help?

During my life I was very fortunate to acquire genuine friends like Harold Campbell, Joe and Olive Banks and Dr Wallach, a graduate of Heidelburg University, my landlady. She provided me with home comforts when on leave from the army and, in some instances, acted *in loco parentis*. Again I pose the question, how much did they shape and influence the pattern of my life and values which I in turn passed on to my children? To the late Mr and Mrs Bergenthal and their son Alec, my everlasting gratitude for their open house and unstinting hospitality extended to me and the 'boys'.

Since my retirement I have been putting thoughts to paper, but a chance meeting with historian and author Dr Helen Fry encouraged me to collate and write my experiences. Because of her cheerful support and gentle prodding, tolerant and kind disposition, she made my task easier. To her my ever grateful thanks for her editorial skills and work in the production of this book, and with special tribute to her charming family for their love and forbearance. Helen was the catalyst who introduced my idea of the book to Sophie Bradshaw at The History Press.

Sophie trusted and accepted her judgement and commissioned me to write this autobiography. Thanks also to Peter Teale for his enthusiastic support and interest in my story. I am grateful to the editorial team at The History Press for publishing my book to such a high standard.

Two other people deserve special thanks in the process of this book: my sincere thanks go to Betty Fifield who transcribed several hours of interviews from discs, and also Alexia Dobinson for typing up hours of material which could not be retrieved from my computer.

My appreciation to the late Mona Drake whose friendship and brotherly love helped us both sustain many times and years of great hardship, and to the late Doris Drake, his first wife, and their children who were and are part of my family. And to Ruth Drake and the late Melvyn Reginald Sheridan (Mendel), whose friendship spanned a lifetime. My everlasting thanks to Shirley and the late Raymond Rudie for their love and friendship. Raymond was my loyal friend, lawyer and tennis partner for over half a century. To my dear friends Audrey and the late Frank Cass, publisher, who over many years of loyal and loving friendship, encouraged me to write my autobiography. He introduced and published the *Essex Jewish News*, to which I contributed fairly regularly over many years. My thanks to Anne and Jerry Goldstein for their longstanding friendship, loyalty and support. To our lifelong friends, Bernard Pearlstone, artist and tennis partner, and Maureen his wife, for their support and enduring friendship, and to my many other friends who over the years have contributed so much to Shirley and me.

My sister-in-law and brother-in-law, Ruth and Bobby Cohen, and Maxine, Hayley and Andy and Ben Newman, for their unstinting love and loyalty. Also my sister-in-law Molly and brother-in-law Piloo Davicha, and nieces Tina, Heidi and Anna and their children.

My everlasting love to my brother Saul, to his wife Miriam and my nephews Evyatar, Amihud and Noam, their wives and children. My sincere thanks to Saul for providing me with additional material for this book. And to my beloved grandchildren: Hemi, Hanan, Boaz, Zachy, Gabby and Yael, for whom this book is a testament of survival.

My heartfelt love and thanks to my dear children Janice Leberman and Jonathan Rothman, and to my dear son-in-law Jay and daughter-in-law Liza (Elizabeth). Their love, support, patience, humour, help and encouragement have sustained me and Shirley.

With everlasting thanks and gratitude to my dear wife Shirley. I wrote this book with her love, guidance and patience. It took a year of solid work which we completed together, thanks to her typing skills and critical reflections. We laughed and shed tears together in the process. Both Shirley and I are grateful to our parents for providing us with ethics and principles which guided us throughout our lives.

1

Early Childhood

Almost from birth I thought I was different from anyone else: neither better nor worse. Just different. Why? It had nothing to do with being Jewish. Were my thought processes dissimilar from others? How could I know at such a young age, but as a child when my parents gave strict orders of 'do this', or 'don't do that', I invariably followed them up with the question 'why?' Then when I started to analyse and dissect utterances which were common to everyone, I thought this strange. Were my parents unlike everyone else? Yes, in my opinion, totally. Understandably, therefore, this supported my original belief of being different.

My father Eisik (later known as Erich) Rothman was born at the end of the nineteenth century in Przemysl, Galicia, then part of Austria. He came from a large family of successful horse traders. At the outbreak of the First World War in 1914, his elder brother was conscripted into the Austrian army. As was common in those days my father, being the younger son and next in line, took his place. Assigned to the *Uhlans* he was quickly promoted and became a *Zugfuehrer* (cavalry officer). I was born Hermann Rothman in Berlin in 1924, ten years after the outbreak of the First World War, but as a young boy I loved hearing about my father's many colourful and dramatic episodes in his army career during the 'lost war', as it was often called. My father always worked hard and unfortunately had little spare time to relate more and more of his rousing stories. Nevertheless, during my childhood, he described his adventures in fits and starts. My mind was gradually filled with these tales of a glamorous cavalry officer saving the Austrian army from defeat. I remember vividly the story about his entry into the cavalry. He was well used to riding a horse without a saddle, such that the change to a more formal military practice presented extreme physical difficulties for him. Getting off a horse was literally 'a pain in the arse'. He confessed that for some days he was forced to walk bow-legged and suffered from painful saddle sores. He became a temporary figure of fun to both his comrades and his family.

Some of his wartime stories had a human touch. Captured by the Russians and incarcerated in a camp somewhere in Georgia, he told the fascinating story of his escapades as camp dentist. Several fellow prisoners complained of toothache, so he gallantly offered his services as dentist. He acquired a set of 'instruments', consisting solely of a pair of pliers, and proceeded to remove the offending teeth. His fame soon spread through the camp and also penetrated the wire to the Russian guards. After that, every morning before daylight a queue of suffering inmates with a variety of dental and orthodontic problems waited for my father. He quickly reduced their pain and suffering with his one and only cure of removing the source of the problem (as he saw it) – by using his valued tool, his pair of pliers, which, I understand, he always plunged into boiling water before attending to the next patient. Payment mainly consisted of food or cigarettes which he shared with his comrades. He soon tired of this and planned his escape.

As he was regarded as the camp dentist, he now had access to the perimeter of the camp and to areas which were formerly out-of-bounds. During this time he secreted the extra food which he had received in payment and hidden it in readiness. Bartering cigarettes and food for civilian clothes, he also acquired a map and other essentials needed for his escape. When the weather turned he changed his clothes, slung his rucksack on his back and walked out of the camp. His main asset, 'treasure', was his command of several Central and Eastern European languages which included Russian, Yiddish, Polish, Hungarian, Romanian and his native language German. It was an arduous journey by foot, horse and train, crossing rivers and other difficult terrain. On the journey home he encountered what he called 'an extraordinary Jewish Community'. It was the Jewish festival of Passover and they invited him to spend the first days of the festival with them. On the eve of the first day of Passover his Jewish hosts re-enacted the exodus from Egypt by wearing Bedouin-style clothing and carrying knapsacks. When they came to the story of the crossing of the Red Sea in the Haggadah (the book containing the narrative of the flight from Egypt), they performed the ritual of crossing the water. Before starting the festive meal, Eisik's hosts passed the plate containing the *matzah* (unleavened bread) over the heads of all present. These very hospitable people insisted that he spend the whole week of Passover in their home.

Homeward bound, he eventually made it to the Austro-Russian line where he was assigned to the infantry. The loss of life in the cavalry regiments was excessive and therefore a large number of remaining units were disbanded, including his former *Uhlans*. Using his own words, 'life was for a short while uneventful', except that on one occasion all lines of communication failed and they had to resort to the old methods. My father volunteered. He took off on horseback carrying an important dispatch. Spotted riding through the lines he was shot at with rifles and machine guns but miraculously survived after finding shelter in a glade. He continued his journey but again came under fire, this time being slightly wounded. Eventually reaching safety, he delivered his message. His feat was recognised by the award of a medal. For a time he acted as a courier, but the losses were colossal and again these riders were dispensed with. Fighting in this area was very fierce. The Russians advanced and took further prisoners, among them my father. Once again he was captured and imprisoned in a POW camp. This time he was not quite so adventurous. It was a bleak period. He had had enough of fighting and being confined; he pined for home. His mind was once more preoccupied on escaping. The knowledge of languages again came to his assistance. Within the camp he was given responsibilities as a translator which gave him access again to premises outside the fence. Circumstances were similar to his first internment and he prepared to bid the camp farewell. When the time was ripe, he took his few belongings and set off home.

By now the war had entered its last stages. Like his compatriots my father had lost the fire to continue fighting. He confided to his parents his wish not to return to his regiment. They suggested that he should make his way to Germany where his stepsister's husband had a lucrative leather manufacturing concern. Decision made, he took his uniform to the River Sarne and threw it in. Even before he jumped on the train, the Armistice had been declared. German and Austrian forces had disintegrated. The victors were setting out demands which would affect the course of European history in ways which could not have been anticipated at the time. In the Treaty of Versailles Germany was forced to pay huge reparations and forbidden to amass armed forces of above 100,000 men. The Rhineland became a de-militarized zone. The economic repercussions of the Treaty of Versailles were to be felt for at least the next decade. Very much later, my father reminisced and said that it could be argued that Austria was made the scapegoat. Austria suffered more than any other nation in this international conflict. The Austro-Hungarian Empire was completely demolished, more children died in childbirth than in any other country and the population suffered poverty and degradation. Recreating Poland and annexing parts of Austria to Poland caused a visible drop in living standards.

My father finally arrived at the Alexanderplatz station in Berlin where he was embraced by his eldest stepsister. She was a slim woman of medium height. She took him to her apartment in the Lothringerstrasse 69, where his brother-in-law Herr Josef Krause was waiting. Herr Krause, a short man with a slight limp, welcomed him into their home. Father never expected charity – what he received he paid back manifold. He stayed with his relatives for a short period and learned the leather-manufacturing business. Often he related his experiences and thoughts when first step-ping off the train at Alexanderplatz. Coming originally from a provincial town in Poland to the fashionable cosmopolitan capital of Berlin of nearly four million inhabitants made an overwhelming impression on him. He stepped forward into a new and different era. In the town he had left behind, motorised vehicles were seldom seen. In Berlin they were more numerous. Droshkies (horse-drawn carriages) and horse-drawn trams were the main mode of transport in his hometown. In Berlin, where the roads were much wider and cobbled, there was the odd mixture of motorised vehicles and horse-drawn carriages, which somehow seemed to harmonise. They blended into the general bustling traffic and crowds of people, all of which camouflaged extreme poverty. Still to be seen were disabled ex-soldiers begging for food and searching for employment. The majority of Germans felt despair, compounded by the knowledge of having to repay the victors of the war immeasurable sums in repara-tions. This hangover persisted during the postwar period and was quoted by many as an excuse for the election of Hitler to power in Germany in January 1933. Has it ever left the German mind and soul?

Unemployment was aggravated by the considerable number of Germans trained purely for the military. No employment could be found and they were thrown on the rubbish heap. The search for ideological answers prompted the increase of Spiritualism, which was not confined to Germany but popular also in the Allied countries.

The relationship between my father (who was in his twenties) and Herr Krause became strained and my father found employment with a firm in a similar trade. Being good-looking, hard-working and conscientious, he soon attracted the boss's attention who thought he would make a suitable match for his daughter. He introduced him to blue-eyed, dark-haired, fashion-conscious Betty. They said it was love at first sight and within a short period they were married. I was born nine months later on 2 September 1924.

My Opa (grandfather), Samuel Rappaport, a devout Jew, made his new son-in-law a business partner. My father rapidly took over the running of the business, enabling my grandfather to retire with grace. Opa visited us daily and enjoyed baking, and every Friday brought us *cholla* (the platted bread for the Sabbath). I spent a lot of time with him. He exercised great patience with me playing cards, dominoes and other games. Often he took me to synagogue and when the time came for the priestly blessing to be recited during the service, I remember stepping with him onto the rostrum (central platform) and he lovingly covered me with his long tallis (praying shawl). Because of his age, his beard and his demeanour he was nicknamed the *Cohen Gadol* (High Priest) and was greatly revered by the community. My Oma (grandmother), Gina, a cultured elegant grand-dame, sadly died when I was five years of age. Mistakenly diagnosed, she was given the wrong medicine and she unexpectedly died. We were all totally shattered by her death.

My parents took up residence in an apartment in a suburb of Berlin: Berlin Lichtenberg. They bought a shop and business premises on the opposite side of the road. We had a live-in maid from Pomerania, who looked after me, cooked and cleaned, while my mother helped my father in the business. My mother Betty, who was born in Leipzig in 1901, had four brothers: Leo, the eldest, was a talented artist who lived nearby. To be an artist was not always lucrative and, at times, he was forced to supplement his income by painting and decorating; Aron, known to everyone as Arthur, was the second brother, the intellectual one who dealt in ball-bearings. At five o'clock in the morning before work he would rise, learn English for an hour and then study philosophy for another hour, particularly Jewish philosophy; Lezer (Eliezer), the next brother, married to Regina, worked as a comptometer operator for *Die Juedische Rundschau* (the leading Jewish weekly newspaper); and last, but by no means least, came Pinkas who was a teenager, more of a friend than an uncle to me. He reached national standards in Greco-roman wrestling.

I was born in the period shortly after the shocking inflation, which apart from unemployment caused numerous bankruptcies. Somehow or other my father managed to survive. He made Hosentraeger (men's braces) and he survived. After all, in those days, every man needed braces to hold his trousers up. Aware of being the only child, grand-child and nephew in this extended family, it became very apparent that I was totally spoiled. This I accepted with grace and dignity. My parents decided to buy a car and I had to accompany them to the showroom. Given the honour to choose between a Chrysler Essex or a Chrysler Plymouth, I opted for the Plymouth. Without hesitation my father bought it.

Father, mother and I set off for Colberg, a beautiful and popular spa on the Baltic Sea. After a few days my father had to return home to attend to his business. While my mother and I were having coffee and cake, listening to music at the bandstand, friends of my parents appeared. They mentioned that their six-year-old son was staying for a further week at a special children's holiday camp. As I knew the boy, my mother suggested that I might like to join him since she had to return home to help my father. Arrangements were made and she left me behind. On reflection, I was totally justified by being devastated and showed great displeasure by crying continuously for two whole days. The management had no option but to phone my parents. 'Come and collect your distressed child immediately', they were told. My poor father drove through the night at great speed and arrived tired. I feared he would be cross with me, but the opposite proved the case. Reassuringly he put his arms around me, kissed me and apologised. We drove back leisurely, stopping for my favourite marzipan, ice-cream and chocolate.

Looking back on this episode in later life, I concluded that the psychological effect had never really disappeared. I cannot recollect having left my parents overnight again until two or three months before my departure for England. In mid-July 1939 (in my fourteenth year) I remember well a debate between my parents and me prior to my leaving our home for Britain – whether I would be able to cope and survive by myself without them. I gave them the assurance that by now I was older and wiser, that I would be going with friends and after all, we hoped that it would only be for a short period.

During the difficult economic and political changes of the late 1920s, people were affected in different ways. To some it was shattering, to others bearable; some felt lost, while others modified their political balance depending on the strength and character of the individual. In 1928–9 my father seemed to manage relatively well and was able to adjust to the transition. However, the almost total collapse of the economy, including the Reichsbank a few years later, brought bankruptcy for my father. Almost immediately my parents started up business again in my mother's name. They worked day and night to keep it afloat.

In 1933 stability returned to Germany and the demand for manufactured goods rapidly increased. We re-employed our former staff and took on new outdoor workers. On one level prospects looked better, but political events in Germany at the start of that year heralded an era that would turn Europe upside down once again, and with it the fate of European Jewry – my family being no exception. Events would overtake us, such that it became a matter of survival. We, as Jews, would be singled out as enemies of the state.

2

Living Under the Hitler Regime

In 1934 there was a new addition to our family with the birth of my brother Sigbert. It had a revolutionary impact on my life. It pulled the rug from under my feet. Relatives, friends and visitors to our home now made a beeline for the baby, totally ignoring the established prince. Gradually, normality returned at home. I entered the Mittleschule (school) in the Grosse Hamburgerstr. I was a keen athlete, played football, continued my violin lessons and spent time with my newly acquired friends. Meanwhile, a different story had been unfolding.

On 30 January 1933, Adolf Hitler came to power in Germany, something which promised stability, restoration of national pride and employment for the masses who had been struggling and had suffered total humiliation in the years following the First World War. But it spelt trouble for Germany's Jews, and within five or six years for the rest of European Jewry. There is no doubt that the National Socialist Party (NSDAP) was prepared for government a long time before they were elected. This is reflected by the enormous amount of legislation passed immediately after they came to power. On 2 February 1933, two days after Hitler's election as Chancellor, a law was passed forbidding general demonstrations. It was no longer possible to offer a voice of resistance publicly against the new government. To do so was to risk one's life. Three weeks later, on 22 February, the Reichstag (German parliament) in Berlin was on fire. Rumours circulated that it was a deliberate plot by Hermann Goering to provide Hitler with an excuse to round up political opponents and ban the communist press. That was never proven, but no matter, political opponents were immediately identified and sent to Dachau, the first of Hitler's concentration camps, located 7km north-west of Munich. Legislation after legislation subsequently followed; too much to enumerate. On 14 July 1933, all political parties bar one were outlawed. On 22 September the following organisations were set up under the auspices of the Reichskulturkummer (Ministry of Culture): the Reichsschriftums, Reichstheater, Reichsfilm, Reichsmusik and Reichspressekammer. The reaction to all this legislation was at first bewilderment. But Germans need order, and they saw in all this new legislation confirmation that the government was taking concrete steps in this direction. Germany was gradually being turned into a nation of conformity, with civil liberties denied, especially for the Jews, and individuality bound to the 'glorious Reich' which controlled everything.

In the early days of Hitlerism people felt uncomfortable but not threatened. Some believed that it would blow over, others watched with concern, with only a small group believing it imperative to 'get out immediately, if you can, and don't take a chance'. They had the gift of prophesy. Jew and Gentile clients felt safe to express their political opinions in my father's premises. Some were extreme and some moderate. My father was always discreet and listened. Even the most innocent comments, my parents agreed, could be subject to interpretation and considered dangerous. Similar rules applied at school. Teachers avoided politics at all costs. It proved difficult and almost impossible, especially in history classes. The unwritten code: 'Tread carefully but safely' was adopted by those who taught and those who listened.

Very early in 1933, I was in my father's workshop where three of my uncles were present. A political discussion took place. Uncle Lezer expressed concern that everyone in the family except him were non-German citizens who held either Polish or stateless passports. Neither my father nor my uncles doubted the extreme anti-Semitism of the National Socialist Party. Uncle Lezer maintained that as a German Jew he would not be affected by outspoken threats against the Jews. He commented: 'They are directed at stateless [people] and foreigners of "mosaic descent".' This was a euphemistic term used frequently by Germans who did not wish to be openly offensive towards Jews. They almost came to blows. In reality, the contrary was maintained. The sufferers would first be the German Jews, followed by the foreign element.

No Jew could claim immunity. I listened in silence to the argument but it had an indelible affect on me. After this, there were no more open political discussions. Shortly after this episode, my Uncle Pinkas and his new wife Erna left for Palestine.

Children have enquiring minds and at times an acute sense of logic. They hear authoritative voices proclaim in the press and on the radio *Die Juden sind unser Unglueck* (the Jews are our misfortune). They see their loving parents, grandparents and extended family around them and cannot understand how this saying relates to them. Questions to this effect were asked in school but the teachers could not answer. They remained *stumm* (silent). Between the children the code of communication was different. Although automatically we as children adopted and enforced a rulebook of silence, at times, realising we were amongst trusted friends, this rule was broken. Unscripted and free discussion brought the answers to some of the guarded and unspoken problems. Differing circumstances required different answers. Had a family experienced the cruel impact of arrest and imprisonment, then language, behaviour and attitude differed and was controlled. Others, not yet experiencing the full impact of Nazism, were more outspoken. It would not be long before all that changed.

As far as my parents were concerned, their business collapsed in the early 1930s. However, during 1932 and 1933 they were in the process of reviving the firm: suppliers were approached, old customers and the outdoor workers were informed and new premises in the centre of Berlin were acquired. Economically they were once again on the way up. The demand for capital and consumer goods increased rapidly. There was a euphoric atmosphere and it was the start of the fool's paradise. Here, I wish to relate the story of the leather belt. No one in their right senses could imagine that a man's leather belt would become a question of politics, economics, ethics and, ultimately, a problem of finance. In our family this was so. Unfortunately, in our case, the Nazis were involved.

Three weeks after Hitler ascended to power the SA, SS and the Stahlheim (Steel Helmet), the Nationalist Ex-Servicemen's Organisation, were elevated to *Hilfspolizei* (Special Constabulary). This produced a considerable demand for uniforms and a large range of accessories. An old customer of my father approached him with an order for leather belts. The problem was not the belt but the emblem – the swastika. This had to be placed prominently in the middle of the buckle. How could my father produce such an item? A heated and animated discussion between my parents took place. To refuse the order meant offending and losing the client, and the authorities would perhaps investigate the matter of why the order was refused. It also meant the loss of substantial earnings, not to mention the moral aspect. At that time nobody could assess the course Nazism would take, so my father went ahead and did the initial order. The real problem started when more orders came in. Another discussion took place, this time amongst members of our extended family involving my uncles and grandfather. It generated into a slanging match. The decision was made easier when boycotts started in April 1933 against 'German Nationals of Jewish persuasion'. Sadly, a negative turned into a positive for us. The problem remained of how to refuse the order. External events came to our help; political laws were passed which indirectly assisted our decision.

The time was 1933 when trade unions were abolished, book-burning took place and the Social Democratic Party (SPD) was banned. In fact, the Nazi Party was the only party allowed. All this now made it impossible for my parents to accept orders for items containing swastikas. My parents had no alternative but to explain this to the client and reject the order. We recommended another manufacturer. In normal circumstances the acceptance or refusal of an order would mainly be a manufacturing or economic problem. However, as said before, who would have thought there would be so many elements to be considered? The world had entered a phase where values were turned upside down. This started an era of insecurity for Jews; insignificant happenings became major or sometimes insurmountable problems.

I soon noticed a decline in the political discussions by my parents. Were they frightened of the consequences? They had a saying: 'walls have ears', and this dictated their behaviour, especially when they met outside acquaintances. Despite hard work they maintained their love of the opera, operetta, music and the theatre, and I inhabited this cultural world. But the continuous bombardment by the press and the radio of Jew-baiting oppressed and depressed all of us without exception. The human spirit does not accept enforced restrictions, it needs to break out. The providers of culture who were restricted by the regime turned inwards and provided the same or even more for their own people – the Jews.

My daily life was full: six hours of school and two or three extra of voluntary lessons in the orchestra, choir, learning violin, shorthand and most importantly sport of all kinds. I remember vividly my parents discussing their elder son overdoing it. My mother's favourite saying was: 'He has no time for anything – not even food.' Food is the top priority for most Jews, but in this I did not conform. I was tall and skinny. As an avid reader all my pocket money went on books and chocolates. In schools, sport and a large number of games became part of the daily curriculum by law. The Jewish school which I attended had to follow suit. Physical training became of paramount importance, and Jewish schools were not exempted. During my attendance at the Volks and Mittelsschule I loved this 'new compulsory addition'. I became Jewish schools sports champion in the high jump, triathlon and sprint relays for my year. For many years I belonged to the Bar Kochba (Jewish sports club) in Berlin. For a time these activities created a protective mechanism for me. It tempered the harshness and realities my fellow Jews suffered.

For many years my father continued to provide a willing ear by being a psychiatrist for those who needed catharsis. Here I must mention a 'gentleman' who on and off appeared in our lives, and I mean in good and bad times. 'K' was a man my father knew well from his childhood, who turned up unexpectedly from time to time, exceptionally well dressed, fashionably attired, perfumed and manicured. Tall, good-looking, well-mannered – his overcoat always slung over his shoulders. My parents called him affectionately to his face a *Hochstapler* (conman). He was a raconteur and my parents, and later on I, listened to his glamorous and entertaining stories – often with a pinch of salt. His accounts of incidents and events were always fascinating. Nobody in their wildest dreams would have thought that political and economic events of the early 30s would have affected 'K'. So when he appeared one day sloppily dressed and the worse for drink it took my parents time to recognise him. After sobering up with strong black coffee he confessed that he had lost everything, including the will to live. My parents realised how the slump had almost destroyed him. He stayed with us for several days, but eventually recovered with some financial help from my parents. After that event he visited us periodically, and appeared fully recovered and back to his old self.

One late evening when the premises were closed there was a bang at the door. When my father opened it he found an unrecognisable man collapsing at his feet. It was 'K', again drunk and sobbing. Expecting the same story of financial woes they tried to console him. To their utter surprise, this time there was a wholly different account of what had transpired. He burst out, 'Edith has left me.' Here unfolds a different chapter. His relationship with Edith, his wife, did not conform to the character he projected. She was quiet and unassuming and resented the image he portrayed. He lived a schizophrenic life – a real-life Walter Mitty. She despised the way he lived but provided a balance and tempered his excesses. Love knows no bounds but she had had enough and wanted a divorce.

My parents immediately volunteered to be the intermediaries. They calmed him down, put him to bed and the next day spoke to Edith. She gave a factual discourse of what life was like with him and she said she had simply had enough. No surprise to my parents. How can one reconcile the irreconcilable? The problem, as my parents saw it, was whether or not to try to stop the break-up. They needed and sought professional advice. But it became evident after some time that their differences were insoluble and they divorced.

Some years later, after my arrival in England, I had lunch with my then landlady Mrs Wallach, and my very close teenage friends in Queens Drive, North London, with whom I shared the lodgings. During the meal Mrs Wallach glanced out of the window and remarked that a lady appeared to be looking continuously up at our window and that she had noticed her several times before. She enquired whether any of us four boys knew her. For the moment we all answered no. Then I reflected and looked again; it was Edith. For some reason I felt embarrassed. How could I explain and relate the whole episode to Mrs Wallach, who was such a refined religious lady? I needed time to think. I admitted that the lady looked familiar and said I would go down and perhaps be able to identify her. We lived on the second floor and it took some time to reach the ground floor. When I looked outside she had gone and so had my problem. Looking back on this incident I feel a sadness that I did not speak to her or make contact. After all, she was a connection with the past and with my family. At the end of the 1950s my parents mentioned that 'K' had escaped to South America and contacted my Uncle Leo, who had found sanctuary in Buenos Aires. 'K' had married again and had a family. He had not changed. He was still debonair and knew all the 'top-knobs'. Eventually, settling in Chile, he dined with the president and led a lavish life.

All of us liked and enjoyed our Chrysler Plymouth and everybody using the car exercised great care. One day Uncle Leo approached my father to borrow the car for an outing. This was during one of Leo's lean periods as an artist. With some reluctance my father agreed. On a business trip to the centre of Berlin he saw a vehicle pass by with a large ladder sticking out of a window. It looked familiar. He looked at the registration number and recognised his own car. He had a fit. On his return home he confronted Leo who confessed, but said he had been given a decorating job and this was his only means of transport.

My father used the car frequently on business trips and on one occasion a car drove into him. When he got out and confronted the other driver he noticed the smell of alcohol. As is normal they exchanged details and the man accepted liability and agreed to pay compensation. The money was not forthcoming and my father telephoned him demanding payment. Nothing further was heard and my father again telephoned. This time the man was abusive and demanded payment of a sum of money, and if the 'dirty Jew' failed to pay he would report the matter to the police. Fortunately, my father had a friend in the police force who telephoned the other driver and obtained payment. This 'righteous Gentile' was to come to our aid again by warning us of an imminent pogrom against the country's Jews by the regime. Discussing the incident of the car with my mother, my father decided that circumstances would not allow him to continue owning a car – it was now too dangerous. With great reluctance he sold it.

In the conversations my parents had with a very small number of customers and visitors they saw the end of democracy. A number of my friends were Gentiles. We played football together and frequently went to the cinema. On one occasion I was asked to go with them to a new club which had been formed for boys of our age. It would start with a short period of political discussion followed by games. They were sure that I would enjoy it. So I went. The club leader, a friendly young man, was casually dressed and spoke to us. He emphasised the change that would ultimately result from declining unemployment, that Germany would once again be respected and find its rightful place in the civilised world. I had no problem with this. During my second visit he spoke detrimentally about the many political parties which had existed before the seizure of power and that many of the leaders of these parties were Jews. I felt hurt. With reluctance I went a third time and only so as not to upset my friends. This time our group leader appeared wearing a Brown Shirt uniform and repeated the unpleasant observations about Jews.

I had had enough. At home I brought this to the attention of my parents. We all agreed that under no circumstances should I attend further meetings. When asked by my National-Socialist friends why I stopped going I simply said that I had additional music lessons. Perhaps they had an inkling of the real reason. Shortly afterwards, all those who regularly attended the club appeared in brown uniforms. The general word 'youth club' was no longer used. Did the children notice the political undertones which were gradually introduced? The word 'club' disappeared and the term *Jungvolk* appeared. It had more attraction for the young who paid less attention to the politics. Enjoyment first, everything else was a by-product. Part of the attraction was the uniform which was so similar to the popular Boy Scout movement in Britain with its activities of camping, sitting around the bonfire, singing and games. It fostered camaraderie, friendship and bonding. These were major ingredients for attracting the young. The group grew rapidly in size; not being a member created a social stigma.

Visits by Uncle Lezer to our premises increased. One particular incident is still vividly imprinted in my mind. When Hitler first came to power my uncle asked my father's thoughts on a Jewish politician named Max Naumann, a lawyer who led the *Verband Nationaldeutscher Juden* (the party of National Socialist Jews) which was formed in the early 1920s. It sympathised with Hitler's National Socialist Party but obviously not with his anti-Semitism. To Naumann, total assimilation was the answer to anti-Semitism. It is said that in March 1933 Hermann Goering tried to enlist Naumann's help, together with that of other leading members of the Jewish Community, in preventing a rally against German anti-Semitism taking place in New York.

A discussion ensued and my father and uncle agreed that any right-wing party, Jewish or otherwise, spelt trouble. Apparently, at a meeting of the local Zionist organisation this item appeared on the agenda and a heated debate took place on how to combat the spread and encouragement of Naumann's fascism. Some maintained the support of this 'crackpot' party was minimal and did not warrant any further discussion. Others felt that it was true the support was negligible at present but it might run parallel with the NSDAP and gain popularity. They were damned if they took action, and damned if they didn't. The matter was shelved. On reflection, I think that was the best policy. The movement never gained popularity and slid into oblivion and in any case it was outlawed at the end of 1935. Max Naumann died in 1939 and did not live to see the terrible atrocities perpetrated against his co-religionists, culminating in the slaughter of six million people.

I learned very quickly that frank Jewish political discussions only took place within a confined space and between trusted friends. The circle shrunk slowly and so did the subjects for discussion. *Jude wohin?* (Jew where to) remained the ongoing and grave problem. Our walls had ears so voices were lowered. And our caution was not only confined to our home but in conversations with the wider family, friends, neighbours and Jews under Nazi rule. Jewish organisations were inundated with very urgent requests to list countries willing to take Jews. When they did, the numbers were absurd and laughable.

The year 1937 saw the celebration of my bar mitzvah, a Jewish religious ritual with a family celebration commemorating the thirteenth birthday of a boy. My bar mitzvah, according to the Hebrew date, was to take place on 14 August 1937, more than two weeks before my actual thirteenth birthday. As my father had decided I should have a good Jewish education, I was able to read Hebrew well and fluently. I sang in the synagogue choir and had additional private Bible and Talmudic lessons twice a week with Mr Hochhauser, a well-known and respected Hebrew teacher. Mr Hochhauser had eighteen children and from time to time I was invited to spend the Friday evening meal with him and his family. The atmosphere sitting round this large Sabbath table was impressive. The table was laid out with a white tablecloth and in the centre stood the lighted candles in brightly burnished silver candlesticks. Two large *chollas*, covered with a velvet embroidered cloth, were blessed by Mr Hochhauser before being shared amongst us. The older children sat near their father and I was seated with the younger ones at the far end. His kindness reflected in the manners of his children who were happy and well-behaved. They paid great respect to both their parents. The elder children helped with serving the meal and cared for the young ones. This portrayed for me a religious model and idyllic home. It was a happy day for me when I discovered that the Hochhauser family had managed to escape Nazi Germany for London, where they set up a successful bookshop in Stamford Hill.

We regularly attended the Alte Synagogue which was built in 1717 and situated in the centre of Berlin. There I sang soprano and occasionally solo in the choir. The choir was renowned in Germany and toured around Europe, particularly in the 1920s. It was associated with the famous cantorial composer Lewandofsky. Our synagogue closely collaborated with the temple in the Kaiserstrasse, situated thirty minutes walk away. Each week they alternated rabbis and cantors, with equal status. They had dignified but somewhat pompous titles of *Ober Rabbiner* (Head Rabbi) and *Ober Cantor* (Head Cantor). Rabbi Dr Freier was a charismatic figure. When he was on duty in the Alte Synagogue he sat on a raised *dais* (platform) surrounded by his young children. He attracted large crowds to the services and his inspiring sermons cleverly contained hidden criticism of the Nazi regime. When he spoke you could hear a pin drop. His mellow sonorous voice vibrated around the whole synagogue, giving comfort and hope to those present. Cantor Hoffman accompanied Rabbi Freier. He had a magnificent tenor voice and his cantorial acrobatics and style complimented well that of the Rabbi. In contrast, the paternal figure of Rabbi Dr Freiman gave consolation to the worried, concerned and distressed congregants. Rabbi Dr Freiman and Cantor Fraenkel were on duty on the day of my bar mitzvah. The Cantor had a rich musical baritone voice. Before being accepted I had to undergo a small informal test with him in Hebrew and singing. He took me on as a pupil and I attended his house once a week. Then started the usual routine: a new outfit with short trousers had to be ordered for the special occasion, a caterer to be employed and invitations sent out to prospective guests. My mother, who always dressed with great style and fashion, spent time with her dressmaker. Business seemed to stop while my father busied himself with his hobby – making the liquors, cherry brandy, crème de menthe, etc. We had a reasonable-sized flat on the first floor and it was decided to have the bar mitzvah party at home over two days; Saturday for family, close friends and VIPs (fifty to sixty people) and the following day, Sunday, for business acquaintances, young people and school friends. Furniture had to be moved and stored and tables and chairs hired for the occasion.

My mother insisted that we have fresh fish as main course. Live freshwater carp and pike were delivered in containers. Naturally the fish had to be stored somewhere. It was my lasting recollection that, by majority decision, the bath was used. For my little brother Sigbert this was heaven. He spent a lot of time poking and playing with the fish and spilling water all over the bathroom floor – fun for him but not for our mother. I shared in my brother's distress when the time came to remove the fish for cooking, as he particularly regarded them and the bathroom as his domain.

On the day of my *brit-mila* (circumcision), when I was eight days old, my father had reserved some vintage wine to be opened thirteen years later on my bar mitzvah. Friday evening, the day before the festivities, guests were invited for dinner. With ceremonial aplomb my father opened the wine and I was given the first glass to drink. The potency of the wine hit me to such an extent that my parents and guests questioned with great hilarity and concern whether I would be able to perform my piece in the synagogue the next day. I shared their opinion and anxiety. Until that time my athletic prowess had prevented me from imbibing in alcoholic drinks. Therefore, the effect it had was far stronger than expected. Immediately, my father ordered strong coffee, put me to bed where I slept heavily, waking early next morning prepared to give the performance of a lifetime.

Forgotten was this incident as I concentrated on the day's forthcoming events. I did not wish to disappoint my parents and, in particular, my grandfather and Uncle Arthur, who were the experts in this field. After a short walk we arrived at the synagogue exactly on time. This tradition has continued throughout my life. Does it not say in the *Shulhan Arukh* (laws and customs of Israel), 'one should enter Synagogue as early as possible and leave it as late as possible'? Shortly before I was called to the Reading of the Torah I noticed and appreciated that quite a number of my friends from the choir had come down from the choir loft to give me moral support. A quiet descended upon the congregation when the *Chazan* called my Hebrew name and I ascended the steps of the *bima* wearing my *tallit* for the first time. I then chanted in Hebrew about five chapters from the book of Deuteronomy in the major scale, followed by a continuing solo performance of my blessings and chapters from Isaiah in the minor scale. My friends then returned to the choir loft and the sound of their voices filled the whole synagogue when they sang first in German *Es segne und behuete dich dein Gott* (Your God should bless you and keep you), followed in Hebrew by the singing of some Psalms. Then came the Rabbi's address in which he praised me for the wonderful singing and delivery of the scriptures. He expressed confidence that I would continue to strictly adhere to the Principles of our faith for the rest of my life through good and bad times. There was a prophetic hint that times would become more difficult and adherence to Jewish principles would become a severe challenge.

After the prayers for the welfare of the state in modified form and the conclusion of the service, my father hugged and kissed me; then I kissed my little brother. I went up to the ladies gallery to kiss and embrace my smiling, proud mother. After the service there was a small reception for the congregants, after which we made our way home together with our Jewish and non-Jewish guests.

On arrival back home we found the apartment festooned with flowers, the tables beautifully laid with white tablecloths, silver cutlery, candelabra and crystal. The Sabbath *cholla* was covered with embroidered velvet completing the decorations. Our home was exquisitely transformed. Kiddush (blessing over the wine) was said, my father welcomed the guests and the meal was served. My grandfather then gave a Talmudic discourse followed by several speeches.

One speech in particular has stayed in my mind by the President of the Lodzer Verein of which my father was the Financial Representative (an association for people from the town of Lodz in Poland). One may well ask why my father was treasurer of this association since he came from a town in Galicia many miles away. For years I have pondered this and it is only recently that I have come up with a reasonable and acceptable explanation. Mr Levine, who owned a large Judaica shop in the Jewish quarter of Berlin, was a close friend of my father and also very friendly with the President of the association. He must have mentioned my father's prize possession – a very large steel safe. Although I cannot recall the essence of this speech, I do vividly remember that the President spoke with a strong Eastern European accent and courageously did not mince his words. He openly attacked the Nazi regime. Those present in our apartment listened with consternation. At that time, foreign Jews enjoyed some immunity which in the years to follow completely disappeared.

The next day was Sunday. Festivities continued on a lighter note with curtailed speeches and more emphasis on music, fun and games. Monday arrived and it meant back to almost normal chores. For those uninvited school friends a synopsis was given of the hilarities and uncensored goings-on of the weekend.

One day, on my return from school, the telephone rang. My mother answered and spoke a few words. She put down the receiver, smiled and told me the happy news. A consignment of kosher meat from Hungary had arrived at Stammler's, the kosher butcher in the Grenadierstrasse of

Berlin. This area was very much like London's Whitechapel. For many years we were regular customers. Since *shechita*, the prescribed method of slaughtering those animals and birds which Jews may eat, was strictly *verboten* (banned) in the Third Reich, only imports were occasionally available in selected shops. Delighted with the news, my mother had placed her order. On returning from school, she asked me to collect it. As I was about thirteen at the time her request was an 'order'. It was a miserable day and although the rain had stopped it was drizzling and the street lights were on. As I turned into Grenadierstrasse I saw an elderly Jew with a beard and sideburns carrying an umbrella. A young boy was walking behind him shouting, swearing and using expletives. This was not uncommon at the time and sensibly the man ignored him. The invectives continued and I heard shouting, 'Stop or I'll kill you.' The Jewish man continued his walk but quickened his pace. Believing that it was not an empty threat, I stupidly ran over and told the youth to stop molesting the old man. The boy shouted at me, 'Jew lover! I'll kill you too.' Little did he realise that I was Jewish too. I assumed he was not carrying a weapon or anything harmful so I confronted him. I was lucky and he ran off, but for me this episode was not finished. I proceeded to collect our meat order and safely delivered it home.

I never revealed to my parents this event for fear of their reaction. Both father and mother would have been furious that I had endangered myself and, no doubt, would have stopped me from entering the Jewish quarter. For myself, this episode had a greater and lasting affect on me. I thought that the boy would have collected a gang, waited for me, beaten me up or even killed me. He would have got away with his actions without any repercussions. There was no justice for Jews. I avoided the area for quite some time and found excuses whenever I was asked to go on errands. It taught me to think before reacting to a situation.

Things gradually deteriorated further for Germany's Jews. Hitler was rearming in contravention of the Treaty of Versailles and in 1936 the Rhineland had been reoccupied. Now he turned his attention fully towards Austria. He had had designs on our neighbour for a long time, which he had made perfectly clear in his book *Mein Kampf* (1925), written over ten years earlier. On 12 March 1938 he ordered troops over the border into Austria and annexed the country in the *Anschluss*. Austria's Jews were now subjected to the anti-Jewish laws which we had lived under for so many years. That summer in July 1938, the Evian

Conference was convened by American President Franklin Roosevelt. The hopes and expectations of all Jews in Germany and Austria were high. It became the topic of discussion shortly before it took place. Twenty-two nations from all parts of the world, including twenty-four voluntary organisations as observers, met at the French town of Evian-les-Bains. My parents and the majority of their friends and fellow religionists were convinced that the gates to paradise would open and hell would be left behind. Someone said that it meant 'a punch in the face of Adolf'. This optimism was confirmed by the opening speeches which expressed sympathy for the plight of those suffering under the totalitarian regime. A number of us read the small and selected available foreign newspapers. The *Daily Mail* was among them. My father managed to buy a copy and I translated some parts which I considered were of current and important interest to my parents.

Unemployment in America, Britain and even Australia was on the decline and there appeared to be no apparent reason for refusing to admit Jewish refugees from Germany and Austria. Most of them, if not all, would prove to be valuable assets to any country. Many were scientists, doctors, lawyers and highly qualified professionals in their fields. It looked hopeful. The problem was which country to go to? No problem for the pessimist, who said: 'to the country which will have me.'

Although my parents usually believed in our great teacher of the Middle Ages, Moses Maimonides, who advocated the 'Golden Middle Way', in certain instances this principle was shelved by them. My mother rushed to various consulates listed in the Jewish Press who were willing to accept a limited number of Jews. She had heard on the grapevine, and believed, that the policy of 'first come first served' was being implemented. There were exceptions, however, like people who had been incarcerated in concentration camps or prison for a period were given absolute priority. A case in question was my Uncle Leo who had been imprisoned for marrying a Gentile. But when my mother arrived at the consulate, she soon discovered that everyone had the same thought. There were queues of many thousands, but she nevertheless optimistically joined the end of the line. The long line did not move. A consular official suddenly appeared and told the many hopefuls that the quota of 150 had been filled; there was absolutely no point in remaining and they should disperse peacefully. Despite this, the pattern was repeated time and time again. People would not take 'no' for an answer.

My father mistakenly believed that a superb craftsman such as him would not find it difficult to be accepted by one of the participant countries of the Evian Conference. Then, thinking rationally, my parents admitted to themselves that the priority list was different to what they had envisaged and, in any case, the numbers allowed were a farce. It was odd and paradoxical that the German newspaper *Völkischer Beobachter* printed the truth when it said: 'It is a shameful spectacle to see how the whole democratic world is oozing sympathy for the poor tormented Jewish people, but remains hard-hearted and obdurate when it comes to helping them ...'

One particular Jewish figure had a more prophetic answer: Chaim Weizmann. As the great Zionist leader, and later first president of the State of Israel, he remarked to Anthony Eden, the then Foreign Minister and later British Prime Minister, that: 'the fire from the synagogues may easily spread from there to Westminster Abbey and to other great English cathedrals.' It was not perhaps divine, as some may have believed, but pure unadulterated realism. The Evian Conference made it quite clear that no holds were barred and the Nazis could act with impunity against the Jews. Kristallnacht, three months later, showed this so very clearly.

My father took an active part in the work of the Keren Kayameth LeIsrael (the Jewish National Fund) and became the chair person of the central branch in Berlin. Not only did it entail fundraising for the purchase of land in Palestine, but also reclamation of desert areas in the Negev. Despite working hard for his own business, my father now devoted all his spare time to the charitable activities of the fund. In another time, when life was normal, my parents were aficionados of the theatre, concerts, the opera and the operetta. When my father was asked to form the Functions Committee, he was in his element. My mother and I did our bit. During events, concerts, plays, variety shows and lectures we showed people to their seats, sold programmes and ran the coffee and tea stalls. Musicians, actors, comedians, singers and cabaret artistes from Austria and Germany attracted vast audiences. These talented and exceptionally well-known performers, barred by the Nazi regime for being Jewish, were desperately searching for employment and were only too happy to perform for a much reduced fee.

We were a religious family, observing the Sabbath and festivals, and I sang in the male choir of the Alte Synagogue. The synagogue had a grandiose chandelier gifted by Frederick the Great which was only lit on festivals. In the later years, when famous Jewish opera singers were denied employment, they would perform with the choir in that beautiful synagogue. Organising cultural and other forms of entertainment served a manifold purpose. The Jews needed an outlet. The severe rigours of their existence meant a desperate need for light relief. In his capacity as chairman, my father was called upon to give references for people wishing to obtain *zertifikat* (certificates) for emigrating to Palestine. Although he could have obtained certificates for himself and his family, he always demurred, always giving first priority to people who had been released from prison or concentration camps.

In the autumn of 1938, my parents' friendship with a local Police Inspector, Herr Belgart, saved our lives. Through him they began to receive advanced notice of impending action against Jews. My father then spread the valuable information to relatives, friends and acquaintances, taking extreme care not to reveal the source. These forewarnings were important because when the Polish Jews were expelled from Germany at the end of October 1938, my father and many others were able to go into hiding and escape deportation. At this time, the Polish Jews were rounded up and exiled to Zbuczyn, a border town in no-man's-land between Germany and Poland. Belgart was our hope. He had appeared in the past as our saviour on many occasions. How he contacted my parents is still a partly unsolved enigma. To me there was an aura of mystery surrounding his friendship with my parents. According to my brother he was introduced to us by our neighbours, the Kaufmanns, ultra-orthodox Jews, who occupied the whole of the second floor. Half of their home was devoted to the manufacture of bedding, the other half was their residential living quarters. They were a noisy, friendly and charming family with five children. Belgart warned my parents of the imminent arrest of Polish Jewish citizens in Berlin. My father immediately notified all friends who fell into the arrest category of their impending danger. A very good friend of my father was the leading recorder of Jewish Cantorial and Yiddish music in Germany called Levin. He had in his shop a large collection of valuable religious appurtenances. The shop, approachable by a narrow long staircase in the centre of the Jewish quarters of Berlin, the Grenadierstrasse, was regarded as a prime target for looting by the Nazis. My father allowed him to store a quantity of silverware in our safe.

Their friendship, so I believe, started when my father became one of his best customers of Cantorial music. At times, as a sign of being held in esteem, my father was permitted to visit Levin's recording studio and make his choice before anyone else. Very early in the morning, around 25 October 1938, I was woken by a sharp knock and a ring at the door. A combination of both denoted some urgency. Having been warned by our saviour Belgart, my father had taken refuge with my grandfather, who was stateless and lived not far from us. I heard the voices of two men enquiring about the whereabouts of my father. My mother explained his temporary absence was due to business visits out of town and expected him to return within two or three days. The Gestapo took their leave. In the afternoon there was another urgent ring at the door. This time I opened it. Two men who identified themselves as Gestapo burst in, shouting in somewhat frightening tones: 'Where is your father?'

'Visiting clients in the provinces,' I repeated in a well-rehearsed sentence.

'When will he be back?'

'In two or three days' time.'

Then they said to me: 'Swear, hands *auf herz* [hand on your heart] that this is so!'

My oath completed, they continued their search. I was not so frightened as I knew my father's whereabouts. With German efficiency they left their visiting cards, with instructions for father to contact them immediately on his return. I gave them this assurance with an unobvious smile of great relief.

A few days later I learned from my school friend Mendel of his own father's fate. According to Mendel, his father was an obstinate man. Although he had been warned by my father's network of the impending danger of arrest and deportation, he himself did not heed the advice but remained at home and was arrested like so many other Polish Jews. Whereas in Berlin only men were rounded up, in many provincial towns whole families were deported to 'no-man's-land'. Poland's refusal to let them in meant that they remained between the German and Polish border. The description of how they were being hounded and bullied is another story.

The deportation of Germany's Polish Jews had unexpected repercussions. The assassination of German diplomat Ernst vom Rath in Paris followed. Vom Rath was shot by Polish Jew Herschel Grynszpan who was enraged by the deportation of his family to Zbuczyn and the conditions under which they were surviving there. The diplomat lay in a critical condition in a Paris hospital for a week, and then on 7 November he died. This was the catalyst Hitler had been waiting for to exact a massive pogrom against the Jews of Germany and Austria. A heavy price was paid for Grynszpan's action. The pogrom, known as Kristallnacht, the Night of Broken Glass, came two days later on 9 and 10 November. Once again we had been warned of the imminent attack by our saviour Herr Belgart, who suggested that we seek refuge outside Berlin with non-Jewish friends or relatives. One of my aunt's sisters was a Gentile and lived in a suburb of Berlin. With no hesitation she offered us shelter, something that was not without its risks for her if discovered by the Gestapo. After packing our necessities, my mother, younger brother and I arrived at her place. My father stayed behind as he wanted to protect his factory premises as far as possible. He boarded up windows, fitted additional locks and removed money and small valuables from the safe.

As our host had insufficient beds, I was content to sleep on two fairly comfortable armchairs. My instructions were not to leave the house under any circumstances and to remain inconspicuous. Our only line of contact with the outside world was a guarded communication with my father by telephone. There actually was no need to issue these instructions, as more than five years under the brutal Hitler regime had made me mature well beyond my fourteen years. During this and subsequent periods, common sense formed part of our survival kit.

That night, through gaps in the curtains, I noticed an unusually red glowing sky. The concern for my father and the successive sound of sirens from fire engines and police cars kept me awake. Jewish people suspected some form of retaliation for the shooting of vom Rath, but how serious, in what form and when was anyone's guess. The continuous noise, the unchanging red skyline throughout the night, plus the smell of burning which somehow penetrated the room, made me conclude that the retribution must be very severe.

At some time during the following day, the 'all clear' came from my father. The mob had attacked the easily accessible and identifiable Jewish shops. Our factory premises were less detectable and may have been thought to be owned by limited companies with mixed shareholding, so they were left unscathed. Our return journey home was a frightening experience, almost beyond description. The windows of Jewish-owned shops, department stores and restaurants had been smashed; broken glass covered the pavements and part of the roads; the empty shelves inside the buildings showed clear signs of extensive looting. Interestingly, properties belonging to British Jews remained untouched, for a cordon of police protected the luxurious department store with the unmistakable Jewish name of 'N. Israel' emblazoned on all its windows.

The next day I very bravely went to school. On my way, I noticed that debris still littered the pavement as the owners appeared to be too afraid to return. The New Synagogue, the pride of German Jewry with its golden domes, was an empty shell. Two hundred other synagogues suffered a similar fate. The school was almost empty. In my class four other pupils turned up and only a few teachers were present. We were told to go home and not to come back until the beginning of the following week.

Over 10,000 Jewish males had been arrested during Kristallnacht; some killed, others incarcerated in concentration camps. I learned that other synagogues across Germany and Austria had been set on fire and razed to a shell of their former glory. The Jews paid a fine of one billion marks and the large sums of money from insurance companies landed up in state coffers. Then the world appeared to wake up and Britain opened its borders to 10,000 Jewish children, the Kindertransport, of which I was one. Even optimists admitted the Jews had no future in Germany and in German-occupied territories. The German expansionist policies were endless and this realisation was devastating. Now that I had turned fourteen, I thought I was able to understand why we Jews were singled out for collective punishment and why we should suffer collective guilt. Even if we were not linked to any crime, misdemeanour or wrongdoing, why was there 'blood guilt'? Perhaps there was such a thing as 'remote guilt'? Or was I still too young to comprehend the incomprehensible? Or did I lack maturity? In the past my mother had always been willing to explain. This time a shrug and a referral to the future was her reply. It spurred me on to find a plausible answer. Was I not described by friends of my parents as a 'precocious' youngster? That gave me an impetuousness to live up to. I thought I had the answer, but values changed. What was acceptable previously now became unacceptable; good became bad, and it appeared to me that the world seemed to have been turned topsy turvy – perhaps not everywhere but only in Germany?

A flood of new anti-Jewish legislation was passed in Germany: Jewish children were barred from attending non-Jewish schools; Jews were not allowed to enter certain areas in Berlin, like Wilhelmstrasse and

Leipzigerstrasse leading to the Unter den Linden; and driving licences were declared invalid. Shortly afterwards, Jews were not allowed to visit theatres, cinemas, concert halls, libraries, museums, ice-skating rinks and swimming pools. They were forbidden to acquire items of gold, platinum, silver including diamonds and pearls – German Jews had to deliver these listed items of value to appointed purchase centres. Jews were forbidden to visit universities. We were now imprisoned behind invisible ghetto walls.

Our loyal outdoor workers, in particular Herr Wald, who worked for Siemens as an engineer in the armaments section, warned my parents of the imminence of war, the danger to Jews and the vulnerability of especially the elderly and children. This warning was reinforced by my hairdresser at the large and famous department store of Hermann Tietz in the Alexanderplatz in central Berlin. He had been cutting my hair since early childhood. Amongst his varied clients were high-ranking members of the German Armed Forces. He reiterated Herr Wald's opinion about the imminence of war and quite openly repeated to my mother: 'Get your son out and you follow him as quickly as possible.' I know my parents did not need to be reminded of the urgency to get me out of Germany. Nevertheless, they immediately telephoned the Palestina Amt in Meinike Strasse and pressurised the office for progress. At the end of June 1939 I received a letter to attend a *Vorbereitungslager* (preparatory camp), set up in Blankenese near Hamburg on the estate of the well-known Jewish banking and philanthropic family of Warburg. Felix Warburg was one of the founder members of the Jewish Agency, an organisation set up for the reestablishment of an autonomous Jewish community in Palestine. Attending this camp was preparatory to my emigration to England, and from there eventually on to Palestine.

I was selected to lead a group of boys and girls my own age on the train journey to the Warburg Estate. Given the tickets, we set off from a main station in Berlin. The first part of the journey was uneventful. Then we stopped at a small town and, leaning out of the window, I enquired: 'How long will the train stop?' I was told: 'About eighteen minutes.' I decided that there would be enough time to buy ice creams, so I took everyone's orders. Then another boy and I jumped off the train and queued for the ice creams. Much to our astonishment, the train suddenly pulled out of the station leaving the two of us behind carrying the melting cornets. Disposing of the undelivered, melting goods in the nearest bin, we were then informed to our dismay and horror that the next train would not be leaving for Hamburg for another two hours. We had no option but to wait and catch the next train, which we duly did. We finally arrived at Hamburg station, not knowing what to expect, especially since I had got all the tickets for our group. I was greatly relieved to find the group waiting for us on the platform, laughing and taking the mickey! My dignity eventually restored, we boarded another train for Blankenese.

On arrival at the estate we were shown to our living quarters which consisted of large roomy dormitories, sleeping about twelve to a room. Boys were in one complex, girls in another. There were already a large number of boys and girls on the estate who had arrived from different parts of Germany. There was an immediate camaraderie enforced by the existing political situation and the first brief exchange between us made this apparent. It became clear from animated discussions in the evenings that anti-Semitism was far more pronounced in smaller communities in the provinces than in cosmopolitan Berlin, and the children from those smaller districts drew comfort from being with the Berliners. The boys talked well into the night and for those who came from the country or small towns, where just a few Jews lived, this was an outlet and a welcome relief. They could let down their guard. We exchanged jokes and taught each other the current popular, and often noisy, songs of the period. How we managed to get up in the morning I'll never know.

The days were taken up with agricultural and horticultural work. We planted vegetables and carried out general maintenance around the estate. In the evenings there was a miscellany of discussions lead by a group leader. In retrospect, I believe this was a sounding board to ascertain our suitability for life in Palestine.

The saying goes: 'All work and no play makes Jack a dull boy', so we formed a football team and played against each other. We played pranks on the new intake of young people. One boy in particular stood out– Bernie Leverant. Tall, blonde, good-looking, intelligent with a treasury of jokes and ditties, he is still remembered today with love and affection. He was a dear friend until his death in the 1970s. Another lifetime friend who became a successful artist was Jessi Zierler, who I also met for the first time in Blankenese. We later cemented our friendship when he and I ultimately went on the Kindertransport to Britain together and then onto Gwrych Castle in North Wales.

I often look back and wonder why one week in Blankenese left such an indelible impact on me. Admittedly, times were out of the ordinary. I had not left my parents' side since the episode in Colberg at the age of four, which was almost forgotten – or was it? The experience of freedom for the first time appeared to have been accepted without visible pain. The upheaval of going to England a short time later was mitigated by being given some responsibilities, meeting boys and girls of my own age and forming lifelong friendships. Who would have thought the impact of these experiences would last a lifetime?

With my time on the Warburg Estate over, I returned home to Berlin, this time without an eventful journey. My parents were anxious to know how I had got on. They were visibly reassured when I spoke about my newly acquired friends and heard my 'censored' version of events.

Now started an anxious waiting period with a problem: How would I be able to say goodbye to my parents, small brother, family and good friends? My parents reassured me by saying they would quickly follow me to Palestine where we would shortly be reunited. As an eager teenager I looked forward to the new adventure ahead. I regarded my trip to England as a brief interim period before being reunited with all my dear ones again. With that attitude in mind, when I packed my portmanteau, it never occurred to me that this would be of a permanent nature. My nonchalant behaviour at the time could, therefore, be understood.

I was only permitted to take one suitcase and I gave priority to my running spikes and a miscellany of sportswear. Everything was packed for a short stay, not a prolonged visit. At a later stage, I questioned why my parents had given me permission to decide priorities for my suitcase. Did they honestly share my belief that my stay would just be for a short period? Would it really be possible to send the rest of my gear in due time or were they protecting me by camouflaging their real fears?

When the time came for me to leave I looked into my mother's face and tried to read her real emotions. Did she really believe that the parting was temporary or did she conceal her true feelings? She put on a brave face but, nevertheless, tears did flow. This I could understand. Any parting of this nature, temporary or otherwise, was highly emotional. But my mother, a skilled actress, still fooled me.

Restrictions imposed by the Children's' Movement meant that only one person was allowed to accompany their child to the station. It was my mother who came. Aware of the fact that the train would stop at another well-known railway station on the outskirts of Berlin, my father planned to be there to wave goodbye. Arriving at the Alexanderplatz Station I joined the group of boys and girls waiting on the platform, all also part of the Kindertransport. Amongst them was my new friend Jessi, accompanied by his mother. We happily greeted each other, looking forward to our journey with an odd mixture of excitement and apprehension.

On boarding the train I saw some familiar smiling and laughing faces. On the surface, it seemed a happy crowd. We children occupied several reserved carriages, the rest of the passengers going about their business. The train pulled out of the station and I leant out of the window to wave goodbye to my mother. After travelling a short distance the train stopped at Bellevue Station where more passengers boarded and, as promised, my father was waiting to say goodbye. I leaned out of the window and he hugged me tightly. The train started to move, with him still standing there and waving as the train left. Some of the girls were unable to restrain their tears. We were subdued as the train started on its long journey.

The journey was uneventful until we reached the Dutch border, where a group of expressionless German officials boarded the train. We became apprehensive. It was known that people could be searched and turned back. Questions were asked but fortunately the person leading our group presented travel documents. The documents were returned in silence and without a smile. We children remained quiet and apprehensive until we finally crossed the border into the Netherlands. Sighing with relief, our happy faces and laughter returned. Much appreciated sandwiches and drinks were handed out by jovial Dutch volunteers, and then we continued our journey to Hook van Holland. It was twilight when the train slowly pulled into the station and we eagerly retrieved our baggage and stepped onto the platform. A group of adults welcomed us and for the first time we unexpectedly heard the Hebrew expression *Shalom Aleichem* (welcome). This expression was usually spoken in an undertone in the country we had just left. But now we felt free.

We boarded the waiting overnight ferry that would take us to England's shores and safety. We were shown into our cabins which had bunk beds; I took the top one and promptly fell fast asleep.

I woke early in the morning to choppy seas and some of us were badly affected by seasickness. Fortunately, I was not one of them and managed to eat a welcome English breakfast (without the bacon and sausages) served by young English waiters. I was deeply impressed by my first encounter with the British, by their politeness and charming manners. The words 'please' and 'thank you' occurred continuously, especially when serving food and drinks. Enquiries were always prefixed or suffixed with 'Sir'. The speed food was served also impressed us hungry fast-growing teenagers.

Finally, we disembarked the boat at Harwich. We had arrived on English soil. The future was uncertain, but as a fourteen-year-old boy I took it all in my stride. It was the beginning of an exciting adventure, the next phase of my life. Little did I know then just how bad things would become in Europe.

3

Emigration and a New Life in England

A train in Harwich Station waited to take us to London. Looking out of the window I noted a distinct difference in the layout and architectural style of British towns. The roofs and chimneys looked regimented and the façade colourless. Yet the people we encountered were in contrast polite, smiling, enquiring and so helpful. When we arrived at Liverpool Street Station, the layout again was so dissimilar to German railway stations. Buses and cars waited on the platforms, quite uncommon to me. Friendly taxi drivers approached, speaking to us astonishingly in Yiddish. Where do you come from? Where are you going? How long are you going to stay in London? And surprised when I replied in English, 'I don't know.' This was my true answer. None of us had any idea.

We boarded a train again and our journey continued south. Eventually, I discovered we were somewhere in the south of England; Kent to be more precise. After a short journey by coach through undulating countryside, quite different to the Berlin area, I spotted a signpost with the name Great Engeham Farm. The farm was near Woodchurch in Kent. It was here that young refugees like me were gathered before moving on to agricultural training centres around Britain. We drove into the farm, parked and unloaded our luggage. Then we were directed to a field already occupied with tents and over a hundred children. After being handed canvas and pegs, we were told to erect our own extended wigwam. Being urbanites, we had not the faintest idea how to do it or where to start. Appealing for help, it soon arrived. A short lesson on tent construction followed and we settled down for the night. Each tent had about ten boys or girls, with room for only six.

My group, which included Bernie and Jessi, continued the close camaraderie earlier established in Blankenese. This meant a great deal of frivolity, pillow fights and the singing of our side-splitting songs learned since Blankenese and well-censored. All this caused the tent to collapse. We appealed for help again, but this time it was not forthcoming. We made an attempt to re-erect our temporary structure, without much success, but with a great deal of hilarity. Eventually – success. We settled down at last, exhausted, to a reduced night's sleep. For the next three or four nights there were repeat performances with different variations. By the time we left the farm at the end of August we had become expert tent builders.

On 1 September 1939, the day Germany invaded Poland, and two days before Britain declared war on Germany, several coaches of youngsters, me among them, were taken to Gwrych Castle in North Wales. It had been made available to the Mizrachi (a religious Zionist organisation) by the Earl of Dundonald and, for most of us, would be our home for the next eighteen months. There were approximately 140 noisy Jewish teenagers of both sexes living together in this somewhat remote gothic-style castle built in the nineteenth century in North Wales. We were indoctrinated with socialistic ideology, which was rather unusual. The original idea was always to train us for kibbutz life in Palestine.

War had broken out on 3 September, just two days after we arrived in Wales. The British Prime Minister Neville Chamberlain broadcast to the nation that day. The country which had offered me refuge under the auspices of the Kindertransport scheme was now at war with my former country, Germany. As youngsters, we thought the war was not going to last very long, two or three months at the most. Then there would be peace and everything would get back to normal. That is the impression we had, perhaps naively.

In the beginning, little organisation and leadership were apparent. For example, meals, and in particular breakfast, were given to us in the following way: large milk urns were put on the floor in the hall and unlimited numbers of cartons, containing a variety of breakfast cereals, appeared from nowhere and landed on the tables. Cornflakes, apparently unknown in Central Europe at the time, proved to be very popular.

In Germany many food products were rationed. In Britain (at the time) food was in abundance. Therefore, for us children at breakfast the sight of churns brimming with fresh milk and numerous cartons of cereals on the table was paradise. The code of conduct seemed to be help yourself to as much as you want and eat as long as you wish. We could not consume such large quantities and much of it spilled onto the floor. If there was a budget, which I believed to be highly unlikely, then certainly in the early days it was greatly exceeded. A general manager could not be detected anywhere. For how long this free-for-all lasted was difficult to tell, but it must have been several months before a supervisor landed on our steps.

Suddenly, party time was over. Sharp reality set in. Gone were the gargantuan milk urns, substituted with normal-sized moderate containers. If you did not get up in time you were deprived of cereals. Breakfast tended to disappear. Utility time was proclaimed. Later in life, I learned the real reason for the demise of Shangri-la – the manager simply enriched himself at our expense. The greater bulk of our food went to shops in Liverpool immediately after collection, and the money from it went in his pocket. It turned out to be a lucrative business. How it was discovered and whether he was punished for his misdeeds remained to us kids an unexplained mystery.

At the beginning of the war, I was still able to correspond with my parents through an address in Sweden which had been given to me by another refugee, Max Schoenbrot. He had relatives there who offered to relay post to and from Germany. Eventually I received news from my parents. My mother wrote that everything was alright and my father had just been given a big contract from Karlstadt department store, one of the largest in Germany, and that I should not worry about them. Whether she said it simply to keep me at peace, I will never know. But at the time I really believed her; I thought everything was fine with them back in Germany. In October 1939 I received another letter from my mother. From the tone of it, I could tell she was absolutely distraught. My father had been arrested by the Gestapo and sent to Sachsenhausen concentration camp near Oranienburg. I remembered what had happened to my father's friend in the camp and I knew this was the end for my father. Now I was distraught but did not want to show my feelings publicly. I took myself into the toilets and burst out crying. The utter inability to help, to extend comforting thoughts to my mother, struck me.

I experienced for the first time a feeling of complete impotence. Thoughts of how to provide help proved nothing but pipedreams. The gap between London and Berlin appeared un-breachable. I recalled the fate of my parents' friends who were arrested, and the routine letter which followed with the request for 8 marks for burial fees. For how long my tears spilled I cannot say, but I prayed and believed then, as now, in the efficacy of prayer. This, I am sure, helped enormously to speed up the mental healing process. Hope led slowly to the acceptance of what I believed to be the inevitable. In order to survive and live with myself I had to make optimism grow. Perhaps peace with Germany appeared a possibility and pressure from the Allies would force Germany to reverse their policy against the Jews. The high hopes lingered on but camouflaged the reality.

I learned quickly to adapt to being without my parents and near relatives. What was the alternative? All those surrounding me were in the same or similar position and this helped greatly. For survival it was necessary to try to live a normal life. So I made every effort to return to what I believed was my real routine world. I received further letters from my mother saying that she had heard from my father. He was fine. Then all communication between me and my mother stopped because it was difficult to get any letters through at this point in the war. I was left in a vacuum with regards to my parents and worried constantly about their safety.

The winter of 1939 was a harsh one. The delivery of food proved hazardous as the higher section of the road leading to the castle was frozen solid. Lorries loaded with provisions were forced to park at a lower, more accessible level. But how could the food be conveyed to the top? With 120 boys and a pick of strong girls we were able to form a long chain, and the loaves of bread and other much-needed provisions reached its destination by the concatenate of hands. There was an important by-product from this – 'bonding'.

Our numbers soon swelled. An influx of adolescents of eighteen- or nineteen years old arrived during a short period and our numbers grew to about 180. They became known as the *aeltere chewra* (the older group), a fusion of German and Hebrew words. Our German past was not forgotten by those who assumed responsibility for us. We had to be pigeonholed. Originally we were divided by age and our knowledge of English, which I spoke well. On this basis, I assume, I landed in *pluga aleph* (group A) and became its youngest member. Unfortunately, this meant leaving behind friends I had met in Hamburg several months earlier, such as Jesse, and instead being together with older boys and girls I did not know well. The exception was Bernie, my Blankenese friend. This extraordinary young man, older than me, and a fluent English speaker, disappointingly turned out to be a loner. However, he became, on and off, a very good and unforgettable friend.

The group discussions were initially rather highbrow. For example, I remember, perhaps oddly, a heated discussion on permitting the 'fusion of objectivity with subjectivity'. This I found utterly boring at the time. So I sought a transfer to group B. It was granted and I dropped the elitist section and joined room 'Bar Kochba', so named at my suggestion because of my long association with this club. We were an odd assortment of eight boys. I shared a bunk bed with Jesse who, being glad to have me back, conceded the top part.

Several of the boys in group B stood out. Most prominent was Schaeffler, a boy from the Chayes Gymnasium in Vienna. Any pupil from this school appeared to be studious, clever and educationally brilliant. Unfortunately, he suffered from some eye complaint and had to administer himself drops twice a day. This ritual produced comic reactions from those watching. Immediately he got out of bed, he took a small mirror and bottle and a syringe filled with a tiny amount of liquid. With his head back, he tried to inject the fluid into his eyes which was not always successful. The substance squirted anywhere except where it was meant to go, or hit roommates who swore. All credit to him, he never lost his temper. Many years later he turned out to be one of my Talmud teachers.

There was a tiny chap called Berisch Lerner. We were in the same class in the Volksschule in the Kaiserstrasse. He was always protected by his elder brother Hersch, who attended the same school, and lo and behold, both turned up in Gwrych Castle. The younger one, surprisingly, was put in my room; the older, a member of the *aeltere chewra*, slept in one of the dormitories allocated to his age group on our floor. He exercised, perhaps quite understandably, rather excessive parental care over his younger brother most of the time. For example, one day he burst into the room demanding information about who had thrown insults at little Berisch. Frightened silence followed as we claimed innocence. His intimidating appearance created fear and it had the desired effect. If a word was unintentionally said then without warning the door would burst open and his threatening figure would appear. Dead silence resulted followed by accusations and a standard interrogation procedure.

New boys came and went from our room without leaving an endurable print, but it was the boys next door who stood out and were in continuous battle with us. Named *dror* (freedom), their group displayed a true spirit of liberality. Of a similar age group, they were full of energy just like us. What else was there to do before going to bed? The childish pranks went on over a period and sometimes non-stop. It became competitive. Water seemed to be in abundance. Doors to the two rooms were so constructed that they allowed buckets of water to be placed on top of them, so that when the door opened water poured over the unsuspecting victim. New inventiveness was soon required to obscure the presence of such deadly missiles. All these games were done in the best of spirits and it helped us to forget our worries and concern for our families left under the clutches of the Germans.

My instructions were to help on a farm about half an hour's walk from the castle. There I found several other 'castle boys' who had started work there some weeks earlier. Amongst them was someone who played a very important part in my life. This was Manfred Drechsler, who slept in the adjoining *dror* bedroom. He was a couple of months younger than me, not quite as tall, good looks, with brown hair and brown eyes, and always nicely dressed. I had great admiration for him in the way he freely communicated with boys and in particular with girls of all ages. Known to everyone by the nickname of 'Mona', he had a delightful uninhibited way with the opposite sex and I thought his sobriquet manner somehow fitted his outgoing, slightly extrovert personality. Plus his charm made him well liked.

At nine o'clock exactly I reported to my new place of work. I found several boys and girls already attempting to erect large tents ready for a scout meeting in a fortnight's time. The lawn, heavily manicured, was a wonderful sight and almost ready for the young visitors. My experiences on the Great Engeham Farm in Kent when I had first arrived proved valuable (not forgetting the many times our tent was pulled down and had to be rebuilt), giving us almost professional status. Perhaps this was the reason why the farmer retained Mona and me. The others were told their presence was no longer required.

The house and outbuildings were in dire need of paint and the farmer, looking at our tent-building abilities, must have assumed we were confirmed masters of all trades, because soon after completing one job our expertise was sought in another; cleaning out stables and sheds, muck spreading, tree cutting, feeding the pigs and laying a new lawn, amongst others. Fortunately, we were not strained, as we only worked half a day – that is from 8 a.m. until 1 p.m. We soon discovered that by staying until 2 p.m. we qualified for lunch which consisted of sand-wiches. These we never failed to claim. The additional hour gave us not only food, but unplanned relaxation. How did we spend our extra hour? There was a lot to talk about. I knew very little about him and equally he knew almost nothing about me. His infinite 'experience' in matters of the opposite sex impressed me greatly and there must have been many things about me which had an attraction for him. We hit it off instantly.

In many ways we were on the same wavelength. Certainly the extra hour went too quickly. What with the additional food, the unusually warm weather for late summer and perhaps an element of curiosity about each other, we were in no hurry to get back. So we often extended the time of return until four o'clock. We talked about our respective places of origin in Germany: Berlin, a cosmopolitan city, held for him an element of curiosity. In a similar way, Magdeburg for me was a small provincial town. There were many clear, and some obscure yet attrac-tive differences discovered during our educational chats. Our learning experience, our willingness to explore wider fields and our desire for discovery bonded us. We both demonstrated, during the hours we spent with one another, that we had enquiring minds seeking consciously or unconsciously to complete our mercilessly interrupted learning. It laid the foundation for an exceedingly deep and very strong relationship.

Unfortunately, as my friendship with Mona grew stronger, my rela-tionship with Jesse became weaker. The element of inquisitiveness proved a factor. Jesse was readable; Mona was not, certainly in the early days. My learning experience about the opposite sex, so vital for a fifteen-year-old boy, was an important element. Mona appeared so knowledgeable for his age, speaking with such certainty; it impressed me no end. His physical and character evaluation of the 'good lookers' could not be impeached in any way. To have his friendship was definitely a step forward in the social and educational ladder. What my charm was I never found out or I simply forgot. If I speculate it may have been my athletic or musical prowess, or both. Could it have been my connection at the time with the elite, i.e. the *madrichim* (leadership) or my fluency in English?

The work schedule changed. We joined a 'professional' threshing team for a short while. During harvest time the team went from farm to farm with an ugly machine which looked, and most probably was, outdated. It did seem to serve its purpose, however. The two men who stood at the very top, that is, Mona and I filled the machine with bales of corn, which were shredded, sorted, landed in sacks and carted away by strong, mature men. Our skills proved invaluable and we were adopted by the team. Although it was hard work, our egos were elevated and, being honest lads, we handed the money earned in total to the *kupah* (general kitty). We were allowed to keep a few pence for buying extras, but unfortunately it did not last long. Nevertheless, we felt it brought us independence, if only in a limited way.

Our childish pranks continued or even intensified. This led to being heavily reprimanded by some of the *madrichim*. 'This has to stop immediately or else…' the command came. It was hard to obey and the pranks continued in a mild, acceptable form. Dr Handler, a medical practitioner, occupied a moderate two-roomed flat on the second floor of the castle. He was of average size, his reddish blonde hairline receding and he looked early forties but may have been younger. Although he conducted his regular 'consultations' by way of visits to our rooms, from time to time necessity required privacy and one of his rooms became his surgery. This was not all his rooms were used for: he also played the accordion rather well and from time to time we held musical soirées in his flat. Most of the time, his visitors were young, good-looking girls, or maybe ladies of a vulnerable age, living in the neighbourhood. They made music together, so we were told, and occasionally by way of proof it resonated inside and outside and attracted crowds of us onto the long staircase where we sat enraptured, listening very attentively. The doctor discovered my 'violinist talents', procured from somewhere a violin and asked me to participate in his musical soirées. This generous gesture enabled me to play not only at his regular music evenings but also with friends such as the good-looking Margot Blum. Her standard of playing was, I considered, below mine but she had certain other talents with which I definitely could not compete. To mention only one, she was undoubtedly attractively curved, but with her remarkable dignity kept the opposite sex well in check. My shyness prevented me from embarking on anything else so very sensibly we confined ourselves purely to music making.

Plenty of opportunities for sport existed. We were fortunate to have a male Maccabi champion with us by the name of Gidi Meir. He was originally from Austria and joined us in the early summer of 1940. A good and strong-looking young man, he held the Maccabi record. I remembered him from my visit to the athletic championships in the Grunewald Stadium in 1938 or 1939. Any record-holder had my unstinting admiration. Unfortunately, Gwrych Castle was situated on a relatively steep hill with few flat surfaces suitable for running, throwing or jumping. The only even part to be found was next to the main building but this only allowed limited outdoor activities. Many suggestions put forward were discarded but eventually the following events had universal approval: volleyball, *voelkerball*, short-distance running and high jump. These restrictions did not in any way curb our enthusiasm. I would have given anything to show off my athletic prowess as well as my organisational skills. After a short discussion, a date and time for events were fixed. Our weekly bulletins heralded the news and made an appeal for participants and organising staff. Volunteers were in abundance and oddly enough there was no shortage of partakers. Perhaps like me, boys and girls who considered themselves budding sportsmen and women, and future Olympic champions, had to start sometime and somewhere. Why not in the grounds of the Earl of Dundonald?

The list of participants in some events grew and in others dwindled. Our organising committee agreed, to my dissatisfaction, to amalgamate the sprints, which left me running against sixteen- and seventeen-year-olds. My chances of winning diminished. Issy Gewirtz, a six-foot-six giant, was years older than me and strong as an ox – what chance had I? I took every opportunity to train hard – as well as taking longer in my morning prayer. My competitive spirit increased day by day and my muscles became stronger, and so did my will to win. The day arrived. There were no starting blocks and nowhere to dig holes in the ground but I had a good pair of plimsolls and believed I had an unforeseen advantage. Six of us were ready. Gidy, our starter, called us in German. *Auf die Plaetze*, then a small pause, *Fertig* and, after the two customary seconds, a shout of *los!* I ran, oblivious to Gewirtz. I heard a sound and visualised a giant appearing next to me. No, it was a figment of my imagination. Whether he had a bad start or I just appeared to be better than the favourite, I won. My self-esteem grew immensely and I looked forward with added confidence to the next round, the high jump.

For this event one has to have a good technique plus innate ability. From past experience I convinced myself confidently, or arrogantly perhaps, that I had both. After a quick assessment I concluded Gewirtz had neither, and I was correct. It was a foregone conclusion; I jumped confidently using the newly acquired, not used by many, 'Western roll', and received my second trophy. For our gazette, published at fairly regular intervals, a full report appeared written by none other than me. As it recorded my own triumphs I could not write the article under my own name as it would reflect conceit. So I disguised my name by spelling it ingeniously, so I thought, backwards. My 'nom de plume' became Namreh Namtor. It did not take long before my arrogance was discovered and it caused me, the exponent of modesty and humility, great embarrassment. I believe Edith Sitwell once said, 'I wish I had time to cultivate modesty but I am too busy thinking about myself'.

In the early days, the ground outside the main entrance acted as a daily assembly square. Every morning, immediately after breakfast, which was served al fresco, the tables and chairs were removed and a roll-call took place. Later, these special amenities stopped as it required volunteers to clear the food and crockery from the tables. No one was available because everybody quickly disappeared. Sorry mates, no more food in the fresh air. From now on, only in the dining room.

On weekends, weather permitting, or during the week in the evenings, the place was used for recreational sports. Voelkerball, so traditional in Germany, remained the favourite as both males and females participated on equal terms. It allowed unrestricted hilarious laughter and competitiveness became of secondary importance. What's more, it led to bonding. Later, I often pondered why this fun, communal game did not become popular in Britain. Possibly it was too German and therefore did not click? I leave it to the social historians to search for an answer.

Some days we strolled on the beautiful shores of the Irish Sea, with nothing to do but walk, talk and while the time away, and perhaps flirt. A warm, gorgeous day and a stone's throw to the sea always invited a collection of youngsters to roam along the beach. I only needed to hear an attractive girl saying: 'Hermann, come and enjoy the calm inviting sea breeze' and somehow I found time. When somebody overheard the tempting, alluring and irresistible invitation it seemed to spread like wildfire. Instead of a tête-à-tête it became a community outing and the whole lot of us ended up playing enthusiastic beach ball.

It seems unlikely that anyone lost their innocence and gained experience, as one or two brashly and audaciously claimed. The only thing I lost was something else. On our group walks to the sea one girl, taller and a little younger than me, asked alluringly to borrow my striking, electrifying and expensive leather jacket. Due to the sudden biting wind she felt cold. Although I did spot a change of weather, for some reason I did not challenge her assertion. Chivalrously I consented and parted temporarily with my prized possession. Spotting my jewel in the crown other young ladies wished to try it on, and I found myself dispensing my munificence to anyone who asked politely and not aggressively. In time, however, I forgot to whom I had bestowed my unbounded generosity. My enquiries, which took place the next day, proved ineffective. I dismally failed to establish the last wearer of my leather jacket. At a cost I learned a vital lesson. Never lend anyone a loved and irreplaceable item, especially for a mere moment of popularity.

Teenagers are continuously engaged in a learning process and energy is available in abundance. Despite working strenuously during the day, time is always found for likeable and amusing activities even until late at night. The next day, tiredness is only noticed if one is occupied in boring or no activities at all. To a stately home such as ours, a golf course was a must, but there appeared to be a shortage of staff for maintenance work so early in the war. Weeding of the links was apparently essential and our management offered a willing hand by supplying us youngsters for the job. Obviously this service was not rendered free of charge. Someone received payment, but certainly not us boys. This remained our gift to the war effort; the people normally required for this chore were released for vital war work. My short learning process revealed that the links must be kept like carpets. Weeds had to be removed immediately on discovery. This is simply and effectively done by dipping a stick, like a very fine knitting needle, into a container of weed killer and then into the weed. In a few days the link resembled a Persian carpet.

While doing my work I met a kind gentleman who enquired where I came from. Not revealing the ghastly word 'Germany', but substituting acceptable 'Poland', he expressed astonishment at my English. He engaged me in a long conversation, momentarily forgetting his play:

'Do they play golf in Poland?'

'Yes,' I answered with certainty.

'Do they use the same balls?'

Again I replied in the affirmative. After many more questions he enquired whether I had played. 'No,' I said. Would I like to learn? After thinking for several seconds I answered, 'Yes'. On his return a day later he brought me some clubs and a number of balls. I thanked him and took my treasures home.

My short spell at the golf course finished and I had to return to more mundane work on the farms. Missing the opportunity to become a budding golfer I distributed my treasures between friends. Each one received one club and one ball. I watched them on grass-covered fields practising a new version of 'golf for budding masters', but in view of missing golf links their interest declined and so did the state of the balls and clubs.

At Gwrych Castle it was decided to imitate, as far as possible, a kibbutz-style self-sufficient life. With this in mind, small satellite kibbutzim were set up. After some six to nine months, small outposts were sought in the area. One such satellite community was sent out to a large estate in Ruthin, owned by Sir Naylor Leyland-Taylor. He offered to make his lodge available to the group as accommodation on condition that a number of us worked on his land. The lodge, a medium-sized grey stone house, was situated at the imposing entrance of the driveway which led to the magnificent stately home occupied by Sir Naylor and his family. The war was on and agricultural labour was in short supply, with British men conscripted into the army to fight. I was selected as part of the vanguard to go to Ruthin where I joined a very small group of boys and girls, of roughly similar age, who had arrived from another hostel on Lord Balfour's estate in Whittinghame in Scotland. On arrival at Ruthin, an attractive young woman, who was about two or three years older than the rest of us, introduced herself as Kaete Loewenthal. Three or four days later, a very serious young man of slight build with an unusual name of Pummi and a surname of Engel (Angel) arrived. Being the eldest, Pummi and Kaete took charge of the daily running of the group. The girls attended to the domestic chores and the boys were sent to various local farms in the area as labourers. At first we were all accommodated at the lodge on the estate.

As the group in Ruthin expanded, new sleeping arrangements had to be found. Sir Naylor made available a barn for the boys. It was exceptionally primitive, cold and uncomfortable with limited storage, toilet and washing facilities. Our neighbours, the cows, pigs and chickens, made quite a din. Fortunately, we were so tired at night that we slept despite the noise. At the time I did not see anything wrong with the arrangement since I was under the impression that this style of life was the norm for farm labourers and, after all, we had to be grateful, as escapees from the Nazi regime, for anything that came our way.

In no time at all work was found for me at a small farm nearby, consisting of about sixty to eighty acres. It was occupied by a young tenant farmer, his wife and small baby. It was situated in the valley with a backdrop of mountains and a small brook running close by. Coming from the busy, cosmopolitan environment of Berlin, and transported into this rural serenity, I became very much aware of the existence of a different style of life. I was the only labourer there. Each morning, after prayers and breakfast, I walked to the farm and awaited instructions. Every day was a learning process. The small herd of cows had to be milked, taken out onto the field and fed; I fed the sheep and pigs; spread muck on the fields and took the horse to the farrier.

Back at the lodge, Kaete Loewenthal had collected a large miscellany of items, for example, pictures from German newspaper cuttings, black silhouettes and sheet music. For a boy of my age I considered this a rather odd hobby. I shared with her an interest in classical music and German poetry. To my astonishment she produced a hand-cranked gramophone and from time to time she invited me to listen to her classical records. About two or three weeks after I arrived, a slender young red-headed soldier of medium height appeared at the door of the lodge asking for Kaete. He introduced himself as her cousin. He stayed with us for three or four days, and he and Kaete would disappear almost daily for long walks. Before he left, Kaete announced that they were engaged and would shortly marry. Therefore, she would be leaving the lodge. We were all astonished, especially me, as I felt she had shown a special interest in me. Before her departure we made a small combined leaving/engagement party. I was surprised when she gave me her collection of 'oddities'; her excuse being that she had so many other things to take and knew that I would take good care of them. Very much later, Kaete changed her name and adopted a nom de plume, Karen Gershon, becoming a famous writer and receiving many accolades, amongst them top literary prize of the State of Israel.

One day, during my stay at the lodge, I was asked to go to the main house where Sir Naylor Leyland-Taylor wished to speak to me. On arriving, he said that he had seen me carrying a violin and had heard me practising. A charity concert was about to be staged in aid of the war effort and he asked if I would be willing to perform. Although I agreed to play, I explained that the violin had been borrowed and that I had already returned it to the owner. He replied that the organiser would arrange for an instrument to be made available. Several days later the promoter of the concert invited me to her home for tea. This was the first time I had been into a Welsh home. On arrival, she asked me to sit down on the sofa and handed me a cup and saucer in one hand, and a plate in the other. At the same time she offered me an array of sandwiches and pastries. This was an unbelievable feast for a hungry fifteen-year-old boy, but an insurmountable problem arose over which hand to use. Should I put the teacup and saucer down? Or the plate? And where should I put them? I then decided to put the cup and saucer on the plate leaving my left hand free to take the cake. My gracious hostess, seeing the problem, then produced a small table for me to use. She went on to tell me of her plan to organise a small concert and handed me some music which she thought suitable for the occasion. I did not think it would provide me with any problems to play but explained that I had no violin.

'Not to worry,' she said. 'When you come next time I'll have one for you.'

When I visited her again she handed me a violin and added, 'It belonged to someone who died from tuberculosis a few days ago.' The smell emerging from the instrument was unbearable and I felt physically sick. She again offered me tea but with the smell still lingering I quickly made my exit, taking the violin and music with me. She said she would shortly let me know the date of the rehearsal and concert.

When I returned to the lodge it was impossible for me to practise on this violin. I knew I could not play at the concert. I related the story to my friends and we all agreed a plausible excuse had to be found. The next time somebody called they were told I was ill with a severe bout of flu. I was disappointed and indeed sorry that I could not appear in the concert and returned the violin after 'my recovery'.

After Kaete Loewenthal had left Gwrych Castle, I realised that I too had the option to leave. My very good friends Mona Drechsler, Adi Hertzberg and Leo Friedmann had similar thoughts. I had a former school friend, Mendel Salomon (later Melvyn Reginald Sheridan), who attended the ORT Technical School in Leeds. He told me there would be no difficulties in joining. I discussed it with my friends and obtained permission to visit Leeds, hopefully to make arrangements for the four of us. I was met by Mendel whom I had not seen since before the war and he took me to his lodgings. My room turned out to be a cupboard under the stairs. That night the city of Leeds was heavily bombed by the Luftwaffe and the only positive thing about that cubby-hole was that I felt safe. The next day I was introduced to the Principal of the School, who informed me that provided Bloomsbury House in London would finance our schooling, my friends and I could be admitted as pupils. However, he suggested a second approach. There was in Leeds a philanthropist by the name of Mark Labovitz who might be persuaded to meet the costs. I returned to Ruthin with the wonderful news that there was a *chance* we could be accepted into the school, so we fixed a date for our departure. We informed our group leader Pummi of our intentions and obtained his blessing.

Temporary lodgings were arranged and about two or three weeks later we left for Leeds. We arrived full of anticipation and excitement at the prospect of joining the ORT School. A message was waiting for me to see our benefactor, Mark Labovitz. I arrived at his spacious, well-furnished office, where a middle-aged man introduced himself. I explained that I and my three friends wished to learn a trade or profession hence our intention to become students at the ORT Technical School. He appeared to be sympathetic and I returned to the lodgings in high spirits. The following day we were all summoned to his office, given tickets and told to take the train to London and report to Bloomsbury House. We thought it strange and felt apprehensive, being teenagers not conversant with bureaucracy. I was unaware that the power of authority lay in administrative headquarters at Bloomsbury House in London. It had the awe-inspiring name of the Children's Movement with overall responsibility for the Kindertransport. Surprising news as we mistakenly thought that it was the Mazrachi, a religious Zionist organisation. (They too were an integral part of this Movement.)

The next day we took the first train to London. On our arrival at the station, someone from Bloomsbury House met us and we were chaperoned to a boarding house in Parsifal Road, north-west London. Compared to the barn in North Wales this was paradise. We slept in warm, soft beds with white cotton sheets and were provided with tasty meals. The lounge, with its colourful carpets on the floor and comfortable armchairs, reminded me of home. During breakfast I met the other residents – a miscellany of refugees, all young men and women from

Central Europe. After breakfast the place emptied and only my three friends and I remained. A telephone call summoned us to Bloomsbury House. Now we were beset by uneasy thoughts. Would they send us back? We had no money for transport and were forced to walk a distance of several miles to the offices, near Holborn in central London. The housekeeper of the boarding house kindly gave us a map and we set off. Being young, strong and energetic boys it took us roughly an hour. We had mixed feelings. Although excited to be in London, we were apprehensive of what was in store for us. London presented an extraordinary sight. In contrast to Berlin, which had varied blocks of three-, four- and five-storey apartments, the streets and areas we passed through had row upon row of terraced, semi-detached or detached one-family houses. They were similar in style but with ugly chimneys protruding from the roofs. For the first time we saw bomb damage. North Wales had been spared the ravages of war and so suddenly the realisation hit us. The war was on. The walk to central London was an eye-opener. We passed through many spacious parks, some with manicured lush green lawns and flower beds, with an array of blending colours, but most of them converted allotments.

Finally, we arrived at Bloomsbury House, which was a large office block not dissimilar to those in Berlin. We were shown into a small office where a stern elderly lady sat behind a desk and introduced herself as Mrs Hardesty.

'You've been naughty boys,' she said.

We then explained that it was not our intention to remain in agriculture, but wished either to study further or, if that was not possible, to learn a trade outside the land. Not changing her demeanour she told us sternly: 'That's not possible. You came here to England to work on agriculture and work on agriculture you will!'

My English was slightly more fluent than that of my friends, so I automatically became the spokesman. Very politely I tried to persuade her that there was an alternative solution and I said the following: 'It is our wish to become financially independent. Could we find a compromise and remain in London and try to find horticultural work? Someone in Parsifal Road mentioned to us that in some areas there are large greenhouses where much-needed vegetables and tomatoes are being grown. The conscription into the forces has caused such an acute shortage of labour, so couldn't we apply for this type of work?'

There was a pause while Mrs Hardesty considered our proposition. She left the room to seek advice. After several minutes she returned and gave sanction to our proposal. She handed us some pocket money and we left, elated at our success. We returned in triumph by foot to Parsifal Road. Later, at the dinner table, we discussed our problems with our 'new' friends and solicited their advice. They promised to help. A few days later someone mentioned that they had visited the Jewish cemetery in Edmonton. The superintendent had a relatively large greenhouse and could employ some, or even all of us. My friend Mona and I took a bus and met the superintendent. We were assured there was work for all four of us, but with little pay. We decided to take the job.

Work started at eight o'clock in the morning and finished at five in the evening. We took the early workman's bus. On arrival we were taken on a grand tour of the cemetery and discovered to our surprise a relatively small greenhouse – there was hardly room for one of us, let alone four. The superintendent realised that four people could not work in it without the danger of injury so he started promoting us to higher office. He explained that the large grounds had to be maintained in immaculate condition and the weeds kept under control. That was to be our job: sweeping the main internal road and clearing it of weeds. Being conscientious workers, we kept the roads and paths in tip-top condition. Leo was promoted to lavatory attendant. The rest of us declined this promotion and continued to keep the arterial roads clear of grass and plants. Leo appeared to be happy; we were not. Obviously the place had not been attended to for years because of staff shortage. The tall weeds obscured the writing on the gravestones and visitors had difficulties locating the last resting place of their dear ones. While the toilets now looked immaculate and brass glittered from all Leo's work, the rest of the cemetery was a wilderness. The grass had not been cut for several months. The excuse given was: 'we have no staff.'

But it did have an advantage for us boys. We felt embarrassed and to a certain extent ashamed to be working in a graveyard, and when we recognised people we knew we hid behind the stones. The weeds and long grass presented ideal camouflage. The three of us, in two weeks, made tremendous strides and transformed the place into something quite presentable. Whether the increase in visitors was due to the improvements made by us is perhaps debatable, nevertheless, the grounds looked respectable and we were proud of our achievement. But this did not mean we wanted to abandon our plan to leave.

When we were approached by the caretaker to dig the graves, we drew the line and told him in no uncertain terms that our work was horticulture and not funereal. One day, we explained our predicament to one of the cemetery employees, who told us that there were huge nurseries in Waltham Abbey and north of the Enfield area. He suggested we seek work there. This time I went off accompanied by Adi to spy out the land. Adi quickly found a job at a nursery in Waltham Cross and I further north in Cheshunt. As luck would have it, the first place I entered, the foreman immediately offered me a job.

'Are you Welsh?' he enquired.

'No, I am Polish but live in Wales,' I answered.

How on earth had he spotted a Welsh accent, I pondered? It must have been the result of a year or so in Wales. Back at our lodgings, I told Mona about the work opportunities and the next day he got a job in a nearby nursery. His boss was a charming and friendly man and we could often travel to and from work together. The work started at eight o'clock in the morning which meant getting up at 6 a.m. With a workman's ticket we saved a small amount in fares. Work finished at five o'clock and on Fridays we had permission to stop work slightly earlier in order to arrive home for the Sabbath. The lengthy bus ride gave me the opportunity to read and study.

Meanwhile, we were still enjoying our freedom and stay in Parsifal Road. We had become very friendly with the other residents, especially the girls. We had come to London from Wales almost immediately after the Battle of Britain, after the summer of 1940. There was a lull and we experienced a period of calm and relative normality. Although people went about their business, they were still apprehensive, knowing that this apparent inaction in the war was only temporary. The Jewish New Year approached and we were invited to spend the High Holy Days with orthodox Jewish families in the area. I received an invitation to spend it with the great and venerable Rabbi Eli Munk, the Rabbi of the Beth Hamidrash Synagogue in Golders Green, north-west London (later known as Munks Synagogue).

Back to work at Cheshunt and I came across two older fellows who worked there too. They introduced themselves as Harold Campbell and Joe Banks. Meeting them had a profound effect on my teenage life.

They were both conscientious objectors. Although I had heard this term, I had never met one. Yet here there were two. Anxious to know more about their beliefs, I subjected them to all sorts of questions over lunch. They were more than happy to explain their position.

'We do not believe that war is justified,' they explained.

'Why?' I asked in astonishment and curiosity. After all, I had lived under and witnessed the brutal Hitler regime that Britain was now fighting against.

They said: 'No physical action should be used to obtain one's political aims.'

This was a new challenge to my young mind. 'Fine,' I continued, 'but if the other party has other ideas and does not respect your principles, and wishes to annihilate you, should you still abide by these noble ideas?'

Their answer was clear: 'Yes.'

'Even if you sacrifice your life?' I persisted.

Again the reply was a 'yes'. In principle it sounded all very noble and altruistic, but I felt it bordered on foolishness. This was at a time when the full extent of Nazi atrocities and the annihilation of Jews was still generally unknown. However, the events of Kristallnacht, which I had witnessed back in November 1938, and the killing and imprisonment of Jews and opponents of Nazism, were well known in the public domain. Harold and Joe seemed to live in an unreal and idealistic world. And although their idealism appeared fanciful, it seemed fresh and completely new to an adolescent like me. A coming Utopia seemed to be the answer. Most people thought this way to a more or lesser degree, but the outlet of their beliefs required a forum. The Co-operative Movement fulfilled this purpose. A publication called the *Comrade*, edited by Harold, had a vast circulation – a figure of eleven million was mentioned but that is difficult to believe. It provided a platform for such ideas. The contributors included many prominent writers and politicians, among them J.B. Priestly. One of my own articles appeared in an issue in 1943.

There were two left-wing influences in my life that have never gone away from me. The first, the 'Bachad' teaching of leftish Zionism, and secondly, the subsequent acceptance of leftish socialism as part of the solution to a peaceful world, as expounded by the likes of Harold and Joe. The basic principle was that unless the idea of achieving happiness by the enrichment of wealth is taught as an ethical imperative, there will never be a world free of strife.

The art of argument still proves the best and most fair way of achieving truth, so I learned from the discussions between Harold and Joe. Then I brought into the melting-pot one aspect that was somewhat alien to both of them – namely God. An agnostic can accept this additional dimension, the atheist not. How to fit this element into their search for truth presented an unforeseen hurdle but was not, as far as I could see, an impossibility. It can be shelved as unresolved, put into a file as in Talmudic debates. Both men, therefore, shelved matters when an impasse occurred. These were sometimes reopened, but otherwise deliberately avoided or forgotten. This was undoubtedly a learning process in my life at a time when I was most receptive and vulnerable to revolutionary ideas. Moving to England caused an unplanned break in my education which required a quantum leap to achieve parity. The long hours of hard physical work often became easier to bear and passed quickly with the extra mental activity.

My days at the nursery in Cheshunt came to an end, but my friendship with Harold and Joe did not cease. I was not receiving what I considered to be a reasonable wage. My friend Adi Hertzberg told me that a nursery run by the Chaplin brothers in Waltham Cross had a vacancy. They were paying between 15/- or even £1 more per week. This was a considerable increase. It was also slightly nearer to travel to each day than Cheshunt. That meant a lower fare, and every penny counted. So I decided to explore that option.

One of the Chaplin brothers interviewed me and offered me a job. He asked me where I came from. I then learned that his wife had also come from Germany, but she had emigrated in the early 1930s. Work with the Chaplin brothers was very similar to what I had previously done, but not so hard. Often Mr Chaplin sympathetically enquired whether I had heard from my parents and I repeatedly replied that I had not.

That Christmas, although I did not celebrate it being a Jew, the boss had his usual party. Everyone looked forward to the 'Christmas Box' much more than the party or drinks. Envelopes were handed to each of us. We all turned away to open them in hopeful anticipation. I almost needed shock treatment. The envelope handed to me contained £20. For me, it was a small fortune. When I heard the sums given to my fellow workers I was quite overwhelmed by the kindness and understanding that had been shown. There was no problem about how to spend the money. The first item on my clothing list happened to be a winter overcoat. How could I have managed without one for so long? The next purchase was a pair of boots and several pairs of socks and underwear (especially *gutkers* – long underpants).

Working on the land meant replacing socks at regular intervals. Until then I had worn several pairs at a time for warmth and also to cover up the holes. My trousers were threadbare and in dire need of replacement. It should be realised that since leaving Germany, there had been no spare money for clothing. Items were stolen; involuntary exchange of clothes took place (never for the better) and wear and tear. I always wore the same outfit for work but managed to keep a special jacket and trousers for the Sabbath. I also yearned for books. I was interested in psychology, and instead of buying the magazine *Psychologist* each week, I decided to take out an annual subscription. Similarly, I acquired other textbooks for further study. It was always my intention to pass exams. An advertisement placed in the *Psychologist* by Wolseley College in Oxford stimulated me and I decided to study by correspondence course. The £20 that I had been given that Christmas went a long way and opened up new horizons. It did not take long to confide in my friends about my change of fortune. They called me a *hochstapler* (conman).

4

Enlisting in the British Army

During the latter part of 1943 Mona and I volunteered for the RAF. In particular I wished to become a pilot and both of us were initially accepted provided we obtained a release as Polish nationals from the Polish Consulate. Here it is important to note that according to German law at the time, one held the nationality of one's father; although I was born in Germany, my father had been born in Przmysl in 1895, which was then in Austria. At the end of the First World War, Przmysl became part of the reconstituted Poland. Therefore, I was a Pole and a 'friendly alien'. My visit to the Polish Consulate was short. As I did not speak Polish I could neither join the Polish Air Force nor the other Polish Armed Forces. By the time all this had been clarified and rectified I received my call-up papers from the British Army as a 'friendly alien'. Somehow some things are never simple. I often wonder how my life would have turned out.

In May 1944, just a month before D-Day, I was ordered to report to the training centre in Maidstone, Kent. Financially, I was unable to leave my work at the nursery and have a break, so I worked right up until I had to leave for army training. I said my farewells to the workers, my boss and his co-directors. He was visibly sorry to see me go and I promised to visit him at the first available opportunity. In my wage envelope, apart from my weekly wage and a further week's payment, there was a bonus of £10. It was a wonderful surprise and totally unexpected. I gave the money to Herr Bergenthal to put into a Post Office account. Herr Bergenthal and his family came from Berlin and their youngest son Alec had been an old school friend. We had both played violin in the school orchestra. I met him by chance in London and he introduced me to the Bar Kochba – a Jewish Athletic Club, which met late afternoon every Thursday at the Sports Field at Skinners Girls School in Stamford Hill. This rekindled my interest in athletics, which had lain dormant while working in horticulture. On several occasions he invited me to his house to play duets, and after a session on the violin his mother, an excellent cook, would invite me for a meal. The Bergenthals were Hungarians who had settled successfully in Berlin but as Jews had had to leave. Mr Bergenthal was in demand as a successful designer in the tailoring trade. He often rendered kindly advice to me which proved invaluable. They had open house every Friday night for young Jewish refugees, including my very close friend Mona, providing dinner and hospitality. Needless to say, I trusted Herr Bergenthal implicitly with the money I received from the nursery.

With my suitcase packed and my account book deposited with my 'banker', I made my way to the train station. Arriving at the army camp in Kent I immediately received my uniform and other gear; then I left the civilian clothes for dispatch home, i.e. to Mona. It was here in the camp that new recruits were assigned to the General Service Corps. All new recruits received a rifle. Being a foreigner I joined the barrack allocated to us. The platoon was made up of mostly refugees like me, an extraordinary assortment of different characters and professions. Some of them were highly educated, having been taught in Cambridge and Oxford universities. The majority were not accustomed to roughing it as I was and found the primitive beds made of strong wood with hard mattresses too uncomfortable to sleep on. The order came to 'Get a good rest. Tomorrow you will have a strenuous day ahead of you.' Most of our lot were unable to obey. I had no difficulty, and although it was not exactly the most agreeable of nights, I slept reasonably well. The ablutions, again found by most to be primitive, I regarded as normal and, above all, manageable.

The next day, elementary 'square bashing' started. Again I had no difficulty with presenting and sloping arms with my rifle. However, this did not apply to a young man who, the night before, I had discovered was a lecturer of physics at Cambridge. Dissimilar to most, he had a slight accent. A little later he informed me that his father had come from the Rhineland in the mid-1930s. He had received a private school education, finishing up at Cambridge where he had been lecturing. He, like me, was of Polish nationality. During our very early training we became friends. I assisted him with some of the physical duties: how to clean his gun, slope arms, take the Bren gun to pieces, reassemble it and have a sly, uninterrupted sleep somewhere on the lawn. He in return told me episodes of campus life in Oxbridge, showing me completely new and exciting aspects of life. Teachers in Germany spoke disparagingly about the two English universities. It was not what you knew but who you knew, so we were given to understand. The picture this young man painted appeared somewhat different. Although he did not dispel my conception of the importance of money, which meant the exclusion of children from poor families, he pointed out there were noticeable changes promising Oxbridge would open up to include youngsters from working-class families.

'When?' I asked.

'Shortly after the war ends,' he replied. The political and social revolution forecast, not only by him but by my socialist friends Harold and Joe, sounded like Utopia in the coming. The defeat of Hitler appeared inevitable. The invasion was only weeks or a few months away. Who dared to say what the chances of survival were for members of His Majesty's Forces and for new conscripts? A lottery no doubt, and its outcome nobody dared think about it. The belief in God and in the efficacy of prayer meant a better chance of remaining alive, or so I reasoned.

The General Service Corps, which new conscripts usually joined, no exemption in my case, had amongst the starting programme a whole range of intelligence tests. We underwent one such test in which many of us scored a high IQ. I was surprised to learn that my score was in the region of 148. I took great pride in that but did not realise just how well I had done until the officers passed my paper to each other and remarked on my astonishing results in the English test. It was probably due to the fact that I was German and trained that way in discipline, which conformed to army procedure. Not being warned, and in no way nervous, I had approached the tests with confidence and in a language that was not my own. All of our platoon were non-British. I realised then that only a small minority spoke English badly. Some may have had an accent, but not only was their vocabulary above average, their grammar and spelling was also better than the average. To my surprise I finished the reasoning test, which was linked to the vocabulary paper, very quickly. However, I struggled a bit when it came to mechanical assembly. The physical ability test presented no problem because my athletic skills came to the fore. I never found out how well I performed in Morse code. Had it been outstanding I am sure I would have been earmarked for the Royal Corps of Signals. These tests took place over a two-week period. I chalked it up to experience.

Most days were spent in 'square bashing', interspersed once a week with parade with the regimental sergeant major or commanding officer. The lance corporal in charge of our platoon breathed fear into us. Early morning he would bellow: 'Wakey, wakey!' and with the exception of one or two, everybody jumped out of bed. Those who did not had ulterior motives. Quite simply they wished to get out of the army. I soon discovered the devious trend. During drilling they did everything deliberately wrong. On route marches they fell behind. There was a reddish-blonde chap who confided in me that he would be leaving the army soon. He did not indicate his timetable and therefore I did not take him seriously. It proved otherwise. 'I shall be out in three or four weeks' time,' he declared. Wishful thinking I maintained. Several times he went on 'compassionate leave'; I thought it was a genuine need.

On one occasion, after his return from London, he said something most interesting: An airplane was shot down near where he lived in Whitechapel, in the East End of London. It had no pilot. In fact, it had no one on board. We all posed the question, 'Who flew it? Perhaps they all bailed out before it was shot down?' No, it definitely had no one in it. Local people concluded it had been flown by remote control. Very shortly afterwards it proved to be a flying bomb (V1).

Considering my native language was German, having done exceptionally well in the intelligence tests and having a good command of English, my commanding officer recommended that I should go to the War Office Selection Board (WOSB) which should lead to a commission. It flattered my ego but I wanted to leave my options open and I contemplated joining the Jewish Brigade – on joining the army I had made a written application expressing the wish to be transferred to the Jewish Brigade which was then fighting in Italy. Another consideration was applying to become a Physical Education instructor. In Maidstone, our physical training man was a famous footballer by the name of Cullis, a centre-half and former England international player. From the information I received, it would have meant completing infantry training first and then applying for a transfer with no assurance of acceptance into the

Army Physical Training Corps. In the end none of my options material-
ised. I finished infantry training and received a transfer to the Royal West
Kent Regiment.

In my platoon were two Jewish boys, not particularly tall, who
appeared to have no obvious love for physical training. Perhaps they
lacked practice in the usual games children and young people play and
enjoy. It showed up when we went on route marches. They found it
heavy going and so lagged behind. This led to anti-Semitic remarks,
primarily from the non-commissioned officers in charge. In a way I
expected this as a remnant of my German experience. But on the other
hand, it was totally alien to life in Britain as I knew it. I never expected in
an enlightened, democratic country such virulent, vindictive and nasty
language. Surely they knew, even in a limited way, that we belonged to a
race persecuted in countries under Nazi domination? This I found mentally hard to digest. But I learned very quickly the semantics of language.
The English people use words, in particular adjectives, instinctively as
an embellishment. True, strong and from time to time hurtful meanings
thereby lose their strength or disappear. Expressions have fashion. They
evaporate, come back and then when used with the original authentic
meaning are lost. This is a character trend common, so far as I know, only
to the British. As the world has become smaller the American influence, in particular through films, television and the media, has increased
considerably. Yet we have maintained some individuality and so has the
United States.

The General Service Corps provided considerable free time and I
spent long periods reading books on psychoanalysis by Freud, Jung
and Adler.

At the end of November 1944 I was told that we were going abroad.
By now the Allied forces had successfully advanced through France,
crossed the major rivers, liberated most of Belgium and were moving
into Holland. We boarded a ferry. It was an unusual crossing because we
slept in hammocks in the hold of the ship. It was difficult but bearable.
We had a young chap with us who could play the banjo. He entertained
us while the rest of us sang songs. Entertainment was very important
because we reflected philosophically that life was not only for fighting
but for socialising. We knew that some of us would not return. At first
we were unable to disembark and go ashore because we were told it
was not safe at that time. We remained on the ship for at least twenty-

four hours before disembarking at Ostend. It had already been liberated by the Allies. When we landed we were housed in barracks, alongside soldiers who had been there for quite some time. They had captured German POWs who were being held there. I approached the major and asked whether I could be of any help as I was bilingual in both German and English. He made the most extraordinary reply: 'We don't need German speakers. We need people like you who know how to shoot a rifle.'

I replied: 'Sir, anybody can learn to shoot a rifle but to be bilingual is a different matter.' He was amazed at my answering him back. I saluted, did about-turn and left him pondering my remarks.

In the barracks in Belgium, life was very different to that in the Royal West Kent in Maidstone. The soldiers I now saw were not the smart boys from training. They had just returned from the front line, tired, slapdash and scruffy, having been through a hell of a lot. The reality dawned on me. This was not training; this was the real thing. Perhaps that is why I answered the major back and offered myself as a linguist.

I also saw the German POWs coming in – their uniforms torn and in a terrible state. What I had experienced previously was nothing compared to what I had experienced in the last hour or two. I saw the contrast between a disciplined life in the barracks and the not-so disciplined life of war. Almost immediately we were dive-bombed by German planes coming overhead, aiming for the railway station or somewhere nearby. For the first time the shock of it was so immense, it is difficult to describe. You could lose your life in a moment. It was that close. It gave me a sense of wanting to survive.

Then we were sent to dug-outs, the measurements of which were about two or three feet deep with a corrugated metal sheet over the top. I was in a dug-out alone. I had a rifle but I didn't really know what to do; nobody gave me any orders and I wondered how long I would stay there. If I had a light shining, the enemy would be able to see me, so I blew out the candle and I was in the dark – quite a frightening experience. I was freezing cold and I thought: how long can this go on? How long could I survive this? Time seemed longer than it actually was.

In the morning I was able to put my face slowly and tentatively outside. I saw others in nearby trenches and it was a huge relief. It was not possible to tell how far we were from the front line, but we heard nearby artillery fire continuously. The firing never stopped; then I saw tanks rolling. I prayed to the Almighty that I would be safe. Then we were warned that the Germans had begun a new offensive: some were wearing British Army uniforms. We were told to be very careful and not to trust anyone.

At the end of December I was moved to a different regiment The King's Own Scottish Borderers (KOSB), to the 4th Battalion. They were part of the 52nd Lowland Division. They had sustained tremendous losses in the fighting and needed reinforcements. This was probably the reason for my transfer, although it was never revealed to me. When it became known that I spoke fluent German I was posted to the intelligence section of the battalion. I met the commanding officer, Lieutenant-Colonel Melville, a truly exceptional man who became like a father to me. I had no parents – they had been left behind when I fled Germany in 1939, their fate unknown to me. Lt Col Melville treated me like his own son. He realised that not only did I speak perfect German, but I was also intelligent. I was sent for a week's intelligence training.

After this training I was back with my unit, just prior to the crossings of the Rhine. The Brigadier trusted my judgement and would often ask my advice on certain things. One day he came to me and said: 'We have to evacuate the whole section here from the area because the Rhine crossing is imminent. We need all Germans to be evacuated back. We don't want them here. Can you arrange that?'

I replied, 'Yes, I will try.'

He continued: 'Move all the Germans, tell them that they must move away from here because the land is needed. The artillery is on its way soon and we will prepare for the Rhine crossing.'

I was still only a Private. For me to undertake this massive evacuation programme of Germans was a huge matter of trust invested in me by the Brigadier. I felt elated at being given such responsibility. It was the first time that I was in a position to issue my own orders.

We encountered another problem. There were lots of dead animals in the region, especially horses and cattle because of artillery attacks. Some of the horses were lying injured. I gave instructions to the soldiers and local Germans to shoot the injured animals which I could hear crying. It broke my heart because I felt deeply sorry for their suffering. We needed to clear the area for the approaching Allied forces that would soon cross the Rhine for the invasion of Germany. I was solely in charge of the mass evacuation of Germans from the area. The advance towards

Germany was sometimes slow, but sure. The Allies were on the verge of invading the country which I had left six years earlier as a young Jewish refugee. Before me now, I saw deflated Germans who knew defeat was imminent. They were shaken, their illusions of the Nazi regime in pieces. Their dreams had been shattered.

After I had finished the evacuation programme, I returned to my intelligence section. There were about six or seven of us in this unit. One day, I was asked by a member of my section: 'Rothman, would you like to come with us on a spying expedition on the Rhine?'

'What does it entail?' I asked.

He replied, 'We have to go by boat at night and report back on what we see.'

So, I agreed to go. I knew I could rely on these chaps; we had to trust each other. I went ahead with the men from my section as observers to a small island on the Rhine. On the opposite side was the enemy. As we crossed to the tiny island by boat to establish our presence, we heard shooting for the first time. I had never been shot at before and the reality hit me. My life was in real danger, but I could not let my colleagues see that I was scared. I was relieved when, after an hour or so, we returned back safely to our unit and reported to Colonel Melville.

A note arrived shortly afterwards for the Colonel, the contents of which basically said that I was to be transferred to the Jewish Brigade. I did not want to go now. I was extremely happy with my new post in intelligence – I had a lot of responsibility and I enjoyed the nature of the work. Colonel Melville gave me some fatherly advice and suggested that I return to Edinburgh, join the Jewish Brigade, by which time the fighting would be nearly or completely over and I would not be killed in action during the Rhine crossing. He thought my talents as a linguist were far more valuable to the British forces than fighting on the front line.

Before I was sent back to Britain, the Allied offensive across the Rhine began. Artillery fire, which started the night before, continued uninterrupted. It lit up the night sky and transformed it into an enormous firework display. The noise was almost unbearable. These were the signals of an impending advance across the river. We received intelligence that the Rhine crossing was scheduled to start at ten o'clock the following morning. Like clockwork, at that time, the sky was filled with gliders. To have a better view I climbed to the roof of the house we were billeted in and witnessed a once-in-a-lifetime spectacle. Unfortunately, some of the gliders crashed before reaching the planned destination; others landed in error on our side of the river and, believing us to be the enemy, started firing. How to convey the misconception proved exceedingly difficult, so we hoisted our sheets and pillow cases as white flags. Ironic laughter followed when they discovered their mistake. Fortunately there were no casualties.

Shortly afterwards, parachutists followed the fleet of gliders, a number of which crashed. A little later we discovered that some were lucky and encountered little resistance, while others met stiff opposition. Immediately behind the invading forces, the Royal Engineers constructed Bailey bridges across the river to carry reinforcements and supplies. I was asked by one of my colleagues whether I would like a lift on the back of his motorbike to cross the river by way of the newly constructed bridges. Not realising what was involved, and expecting a fairly comfortable ride, I said yes. Planks were missing and our motorbike was more in flight than on the ground. I felt like one of the first commandos across but without being fired at. We made it unscathed.

A day or so later the sun was shining and I decided to relax and sit outside our headquarters. The peace was disturbed by the arrival of an armoured vehicle. The turret opened and a head popped out. I recognised the gentleman immediately. It was Prime Minister Winston Churchill visiting the front line. He asked me whether the general commanding the division was available. After checking inside I reported, 'No.' Mr Churchill replied, 'When he returns, please tell him that I've called.' That I did.

Given short leave I decided to go to Brussels. The war was by no means finished. In the distance I watched the V2 rockets being launched – some reaching targets in England, others failing and falling short. The population in Belgium was despondent. They felt the war was never-ending and blamed the Allies. Discontentment and unwarranted criticism fell on the one-time liberators. They seemed to forget that Britain too had suffered for a long time dreadful hardship, loss of life by the destruction of towns and villages by the Luftwaffe and V1s and V2s, and enormous losses by the men fighting to liberate Europe.

I finally returned to Edinburgh just before VE Day, 8 May 1945. The war was over. I felt elated that the Nazi regime had been defeated. But much work still lay ahead for the Allied occupying forces. I was selected to take part in the Victory Parade in the Scottish capital. The people of

Edinburgh lined the streets. We marched through the city and along Princes Street with the bagpipes playing. As I took part in full uniform I felt proud to be a British soldier, but also grateful to the Almighty that my life had been spared because the things that I had seen at times during the war were very frightening.

After VE Day I was informed that I was being posted to the interpreters' school in Brussels. I arrived in Farnborough in the south of England ready for my flight to Brussels. I was directed by a young soldier to an extremely primitive Nissen hut – a dozen metal beds, each with an uncomfortable mattress and pillow, little space to hang one's clothes and dull lighting. It was in stark contrast to the comparative 'luxury' I had enjoyed in London just weeks before.

The dismal weather added to a feeling of an unusual depression. Perhaps this was triggered by the uncertainty or ignorance of what lay ahead. This uncertainty must have been a common psychological affliction that many suffered from at that time, or so I consoled myself. How scenery can change in a flash. The door opened and in walked my old friend Mendel. I had only seen him a few days earlier at a party. The primitive accommodation suddenly became more bearable.

That evening our spirits were lifted further by an unexpected performance of *Private Lives* by the Royal Shakespeare Company. As I had not seen many stage performances of plays before, it turned out to be a memorable evening, and more than compensated for our poor accommodation. The next day the sun was shining, and I drew fresh energy from the wonderful experience of the previous night.

The flight to Brussels was delayed for a further day, but since the weather was beautiful I took a stroll, filling my lungs with much-needed fresh air. I then packed my few belongings and waited for instructions to board the plane. This was my first flight and understandably there was, to put it mildly, apprehension. I took my prayer book and recited psalms. Mendel and I were then shown to the rear of the aircraft which turned out to be a Lancaster Bomber. There were few seats on the bomber. I put my kitbag aside and sat down near the rear-gunner's seat ready for take off. I mumbled a few prayers again. I was scared but tried not to show it because it seemed unmanly. The plane took off. Once we had reached a reasonable height there was a scramble for the rear-gunner's seat. Politely I gave way to Mendel who fearlessly climbed into the turret, pressed a button and swivelled round. After a while he offered the seat to me; at first I declined, but for fear of being accused of cowardice I sat in the seat briefly and then offered it to any interested party. Everyone politely refused except Mendel, who placed himself back into the turret. After I thought he looked secure, I pressed the button which swivelled him round to the amusement of all of us watching. Unperturbed he gave the impression of enjoying it. The flight was short and uneventful. We landed in an airport near Brussels. British soldiers, emaciated and recently released from German POW camps, were waiting to board our plane which was due to return to London.

There was a manifest pessimism in Belgium. People hoping to discover relatives and friends looked noticeably disappointed. Happy faces from some and despair from others. The search for survivors continued unabated. I strolled down the Bois de Bolognes where there was an open-air tea dance in progress. It was exceptionally crowded for a weekday. The dance floor attracted many people but far more were milling around the dancers, talking heatedly, shouting at times and gesticulating. I found this odd and I made a polite enquiry of what was going on. My knowledge of German and Yiddish proved helpful. All was soon revealed. It turned out to be an unusual exchange for 'lost and found human beings'. Those Belgians who had been taken by the Nazis for forced labour, or incarcerated in concentration camps, were now being searched for by their relatives. This encouraged auxiliary enterprises such as the Black Market and money traders. The Bois became a hive of industry and commerce and temporarily replaced the stock exchange. I took advantage of the available facilities and enquired about the fate of a number of very good school friends. Ruben Dratwa came to mind. 'No problem,' said someone pointing to a crowded table. 'He is the gentleman taking today's court session.'

I advanced cautiously. I had no difficulty in recognising my old friend who was now seemingly busy with a business transaction. He spotted me and left his clientele, running towards me. The joy of meeting him alive was unbelievable. We both cried unashamedly. He shouted to someone and a pleasant young girl appeared who called me Hermann. She embraced and kissed me. It was his sister. I told him that Mendel was also alive and explained that we were at the interpreters' school not far from the Bois. He invited both of us to his home for a meal, but we accepted with mixed feelings. Obviously as a camp survivor he must be short of money and food. We felt it only appropriate to invite him and his sister for a meal first. After making enquiries, we found a first-class restaurant serving excellent gourmet food at reasonable prices. The invitation was accepted and during the meal we heard a not-unfamiliar story of flight from home, being caught by the Nazis, internment in a concentration camp and near death by starvation. Dratwa told us of death marches for many hundreds of miles to safety and then back to Brussels – there was no sign of his parents, presumed dead.

Belgium was an enigma. I was astonished at the delicacies which were available in shops. Confectionaries such as milk chocolate, marzipan, praline and crystallised fruit (which I had not seen for years) could not only be seen in shop windows but were for sale. Certainly they were not cheap, but at least they were there for purchase. The situation was very different over the border in France and Holland where people were starving. There was little food to purchase and people, in particular children, begged for food. After enquiring about the difference I was given a number of explanations, none of which I could fully understand at the time. I accepted the anomaly without further question.

The day of Dratwa's invitation arrived. Mendel and I had stashed away our small rations of plain chocolate ready for a special occasion. Off we went in style by taxi, displaying our affluence. The exterior of the house where Dratwa was staying was surprisingly pleasant. We concluded it must have been rented at a reasonable price to victims of Nazi persecution. Similarly, the interior was furnished with impressive, tasteful furniture, not dissimilar to our own house in Berlin in the 1930s. On the dining-room table was a bowl filled to the brim with a selection of fruit that I had not seen for many years. The large sideboard had a display of the most exquisite china and porcelain. In a smaller antique cabinet there were many striking silver pieces and on a small table was a glass dish containing confectionary not seen since before the war. We decided to hold back our collected assortment of 'utility' chocolates to save us embarrassment.

We had a wonderful evening with Dratwa. Whenever we subsequently saw him, he always had an entourage around him. Business associates? I suggested to Mendel that we should give him business by exchanging our English currency through him. We collected our few pounds and, after telling his associates the reason for wanting to speak to him, we were admitted to his sanctum.

'How much?' he asked.

We told him. He laughed quietly and diplomatically, apparently not to embarrass us. His associates dealt with our 'consignment'. On our way out we saw huge bundles of notes passing hands and we got the picture. Out of friendship we saw him several times after that, when he invited us for a meal and drink in some exclusive places where he was well known and respected. His zest for money was obvious and natural and could easily be explained. 'Live for today, you never know what tomorrow has in store for you' appeared to be his general motto, like for so many camp survivors. On reflection, I should have kept in contact with him for 'old times' sake', but I was too preoccupied, perhaps very selfishly, with my own affairs and my 'great expectations': a personal Utopia many dreamed of at the time, including me.

This was not only a monopoly of the young. The common yearnings for a better world, only fools did not share. This was not a pipedream but the reality of the day. Looking back now, it was unreal – more of a fool's paradise. The realities of yesterday became the foolishness of today. Holocaust survivors either completely lost their faith or became stronger in their belief. A little later, when meeting many more inmates of Bergen-Belsen concentration camp, this phenomenon was more strongly noticeable.

Waiting for the interpreters' school to commence was a lesson in passing the time meaningfully and with the minimum of expense. The forces club in Brussels lacked cultural activities, unless tea dances are classified as a form of culture. Not that I objected to this kind of 'cultural' outlet.

Our daily morning routine had a military flavour. After all, we were still in the army and could not forget it. The smartest was selected to be 'stick orderly' to the commanding officer. It meant appearing at morning parade with a short haircut, smartly dressed, shoes polished to the extreme and cleanly shaven. A special effort was required from all of us. The object was clear that even in peacetime discipline must be maintained at all cost. I was selected, given a red sash, remained in the army precincts for an hour and then dashed off free to roam in Brussels.

Short of money, my friends and I designed an ingenious scheme. Boarding a train we were equipped with our 'liquor card'. It showed the dates of our entitlement to cheap whisky, gin and free cigarettes. The privilege was strictly monitored by the issue of a card which was stamped and looked very official. Shown at the railway station or on the train, this impressive piece of paper gave free first-class travel to almost everywhere. For the moment it was more than adequate for local travel. At that time it seemed that English was still a language spoken and understood by a selective few, and the Germans had left their mark on European culture by the introduction of heavily stamped documents and papers. This gave everything the sign of authenticity and served us well. There was proof that paupers like me and kindred spirits can survive through ingenuity.

The weeks went by very quickly and school, with preliminary tests, started. No difficulties were experienced in German but my rustiness in French showed through very quickly and I asked politely to be withdrawn from classes. This was gratefully accepted. I do remember vividly the first papers for translation: A patient was admitted to hospital and examination showed he suffered from multiple undiagnosed fractures followed by a long detailed description of suspected illnesses. In truth, a year's study at medical school would have been helpful or at the very least use of an English/German medical dictionary. This scenario was followed by a breakdown on the railway. Again here, a technical knowledge of railway engineering would have been of benefit. Some boys admitted no difficulties and appeared to have an encyclopaedic knowledge of both rail mechanics and medical pathology. I had neither and blamed my parents for their elementary neglect but struggled on and prayed for some subjects where I had an expert knowledge.

I heard that some of my fellow students had worked as translators and interpreters at the League of Nations in Geneva and they gave me a demonstration of how to translate painlessly and with speed from one language to another. To them it was automatic and came with continued practice. Indeed, I was grateful for their guidance and lessons in technique, and I acquired a degree of proficiency in translation during the fortnight I spent on the course.

Through the grapevine I had heard, before I went on the course, that anyone who could ride a motorbike received one. Mendel and I put our names down. Meanwhile, I took a lesson from a young Dane I had befriended who gave me theoretical instructions. I was given a Matchless 350 and started it without difficulties. Somehow, after releasing the clutch, it stalled. I drew the instructor's attention to it. He started it immediately and maintained he could not find a mechanical fault. I tried again and again. No success. Embarrassed to approach him once more, I sought help from my Danish friend who explained that I released the clutch too fast. Success at last. I drove away but without control and it behaved like a young stallion. How to tame this beast? Again I sought outside help but, before I could do so, I crashed into a garden fence, fortunately without causing myself any physical damage – only the poor bike suffered. No problem I was assured. Take another one, and so I did. The beast was controlled by now and we became inseparable. Mendel was not so lucky (he never seemed to be). No Matchless models were available for him and he ended up with an Ariel. After his first breakdown, no replacement was available and he had to practice on borrowed models.

A week later we went on an outing to Blankenberg. This was one of the proficiency tests. We set out, ten of us, early on a Sunday morning. Strange as it may seem, our two instructors advised us very oddly to fortify ourselves with beer. Although I very rarely drank, simply because it had no appeal to me, we were told that it was an 'order'. In those days it appeared not to be an offence to fortify oneself with an alcoholic beverage. As the riding instructors confined themselves to a drink or two we blindly followed. At regular intervals we stopped 'to top up'. It made everyone fearless, some without realising it. Certainly I was oblivious to the speed we were travelling at but my pride was at stake. I desperately tried to keep up with the leaders of the troop. All of a sudden, alarm bells rang. One of our convoy was on fire. We stopped abruptly to investigate. It was none other than Mendel's Ariel which was burning fiercely. He was told to move away quickly for fear of explosion. This he did but after that he was unable to continue. The necessary arrangements were made for him to return by bus and the bike to be collected.

Meanwhile, the rest of us continued at an excessive speed so as not to miss our absolutely vital lunch. This was washed down with some more alcoholic liquid. It led to an exchange of war reminiscences and a return to barracks but not before splicing the main brace and testing the maximum speed of the motorcycles which was in the region of 88mph. Undoubtedly I aspired temporarily to become a fearless racing driver. Nevertheless, another vehicle was found for Mendel and we continued our progress to become better interpreters; and in between we indulged in square-bashing followed by the innocent pleasures of tea dancing.

The end of the European war brought with it an atmosphere of euphoria. The celebrations lasted longer so as to make up for the long war years of deprivation. To have survived not only the slaughter on the battlefields, in the air or at sea, the trauma of bombing and for my people the additional pain of the atrocious, hellish Holocaust, meant experiencing a miracle. Paradise was born with a guarantee to last for an eternity. Many things were taken from me but, with the innocence of youth, I believed they would be restored with interest. During the early part of the war I had corresponded irregularly with my uncle Pinkas Rappaport, who had emigrated with his wife Erna to Palestine in 1933. He had volunteered for the Palestine Regiment shortly after the beginning of the war and served side by side with the British Army in Tobruk. In late 1941 to early 1942, through my Aunt Erna, I had heard of the miraculous escape from Germany and safe arrival in Acre near Haifa of my mother and brother. I still had no news of my father. But my mother and I had corresponded as regularly as possible after that.

By the end of the war we had news of my father's internment in the southern part of Italy, but I was lucky to have my parents and brother alive; this was more than many of my friends had, who were now searching with increased vigour for survivors in their own family, often with ravaging results. My best friend Mona heard that his mother was alive in Theresienstadt. There was elation. Further research revealed that towards the end of the war she was moved to Auschwitz. Frantic enquiries began by phone and in writing, lasting an eternity it seemed. It transpired that her death had occurred shortly before the liberation of the camp; how truly terrible for my friend. The first feelings of great hope were plunged into devastating despair and this was a common pattern for so many.

My time at the interpreters' school came to an end. My posting was to be the headquarters of the Intelligence Corps in Bad Salzuflen. Unfortunately, Mendel and I were separated and he was sent to the Ruhr area in a mine detection unit. My motorbike proved to be invaluable. It was an independent form of transport. With no hurry to report, I roamed around Belgium for a while, visiting old and new friends and acquaintances. With two stripes on my arm there was now great respectability and with it responsibility, so I thought mistakenly. I learned a lifelong lesson very quickly: it is the man that counts and not so much his outward appearance or what he believes he is. At its best it is an overemphasis of what one is or what one believes one is. At its worst it is megalomania, often only in a mild form and fortunately curable. Sometimes it lingers on for a while.

After my short, not particularly adventurous tour I arrived in Bad Salzuflen and was shown my new abode. The converted small barracks, houses and villas which formed our headquarters were comfortable. There was a short waiting period which gave time for a mental review of the last few months. I made friends with Henry Howard Marcel Roberts and Ralph Parker. Henry had a very stylish, impressive name and he believed he had to give effect to his aristocratic name by his behaviour. He was of medium height, dark-haired with brown eyes and a small hook nose. By some members of the opposite sex he was regarded as good-looking.

Without perhaps realising it he proved to be my cultural tutor and guide for a period. No one I had known before had such unparalleled knowledge of classical music. I was very impressed with him. Any route march became an educational exercise. To relieve the boredom we instituted quiz time. Mozart was definitely his favourite. There were no restrictions to movements of a symphony, all received rendering. Amazingly, many melodies sung then remain in my memory to this day, and it is difficult to tell whether it was Henry's influence that made me consider a musical career later in life. Young people need a role model from time to time and looking back he filled this position admirably. His education was not restricted to the cultural sphere. He refrained from talking about his sexual excursions but purely for my enlightenment and for the advancement of my education, he gave me some illustrations of what to do and what not to do. I promised faithfully to keep everything in the strictest confidence. This invaluable material was indelibly imprinted in my mind, incorporated in my mental textbook and referred to at various intervals.

Another member of our group was Peter Blake. I shared a room with him. Unlike me, he was completely irreligious, assimilated and unpretentious. Opposites attract and we respected each other's differences. I also believe, even though he had discarded his Jewish religion, that there was a categorical imperative which prevented him from discharging it completely. His father, whom I had met, was also an assimilated Jew but, as with many others like him, was unable to abandon his Jewishness completely. Peter had abandoned his accent almost entirely but, as with all of us from time to time, we lapsed into the vernacular of the country of our birth, especially when in a temper. Peter was also a skilful educator.

Shortly afterwards, I was posted to Westertimke in Germany, between Hamburg and Bremen, for the next stage of my duties with the Intelligence Corps. This would turn out to be an extraordinary course of events and would involve me in top secret duties.

1. Myself, Herman Rothman.

2. My father Erich serving in the Austrian Army in the First World War.

3. Myself, at two years old.

4. My maternal grandmother Gina Rappaport with friends in Karlsbad, then Czechoslovakia.

5. My paternal grandfather Joseph Rothman.

6. My maternal great-grandfather
Saul Rappaport.

7. My grandmother Gina
Rappaport with Uncle Leo.

Above: 8. *Back row:* My father and me; *front row:* My brother Sigbert (later Saul), my maternal grandfather and my mother. Above

9. As a young boy with my parents.

10. Erich Rothman with friends.

11. With my parents and Uncle Pinkus.

12. With my mother and younger brother.

13. My mother Betty.

14. Sports training, Parliament Hill Fields, Hampstead, North-West London, 1943.

15. My friend Mona Drechsler (later Drake).

*Above:*16. *From left to right:* Mendel (Melvyn Reginald Sheridan), me and Max Steinfeld, Brussels, 1945.

17. In Westertimke, Germany, 1945.

Below: 18. My business card.

Mr. H. ROTHMAN
Intelligence Section
MÜNCHEN-GLADBACH

Tel. M.-Gladbach 5063 private 5082
Krefeld 29 155
29 154
29 105

Office: M.-GLADBACH
Gneisenaustr. 44
KREFELD
MILGOV building

19. The office in Fallingbostel where I translated Goebbels' Addendum to Hitler's Will.

20. Posing with my Matchless 350 motorbike in Brussels, June 1945.

21. *Back row from left to right:* Henry Roberts and Ralph Parker; *front row:* Myself in between two members of staff, Fallingbostel, 1945.

22. 3rd British Counter-Intelligence Section, Fallingbostel, 1945.

23. In Bruges, Belgium, 1945.

24. In the Ruhr, Germany, in the Intelligence Section of the British Control Commission.

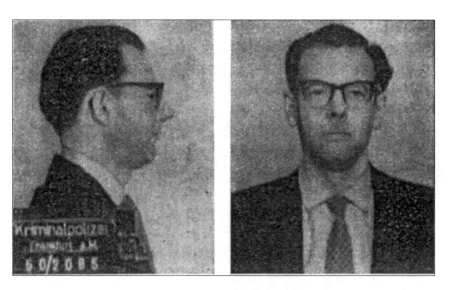

25. Perry Broad at the Frankfurt Auschwitz Trial, 1964.

26. With my future wife Shirley.

27. Our wedding day.

28. Myself in 2001.

29. Shirley in 2001.

30. Meeting King Hussein of Jordan when I was a Governor at King Solomon School, Barkingside, Essex. Sir Alan Sugar is standing on the left behind the King.

31. With our children, their spouses and all our grandchildren at a family bar mitzvah party of grandson Hemi Leberman.

5

Westertimke and Fallingbostel

Leaving Bad Salzuflen by motorbike, I travelled north to Bremerhaven and then west to an outlandish place called Westertimke. The village I arrived at was clean but ordinary. I was provided with decent and acceptable accommodation. I looked forward to my first major assignment after leaving the interpreters' school with a slight feeling of apprehension. I wondered what the job would be like. I was not so much worried about responsibility but about my duties and the people I was going to be with. The next day I made my way to an uninhabited area searching for barracks occupied by former imprisoned British Army personnel. I found what looked like deserted and forlorn army huts; why was my presence so urgently needed in this dump, I asked myself.

To my utter astonishment there was snow on the ground. But it was summertime. I saw British soldiers running about half-naked, covered with bandages from head to foot, being chased by German soldiers. There were shouts in English with moderate obscenities and loud shots of pistols firing. This was followed by indistinct commands in German and people falling to the ground with expressions of anger interspersed with swearing. I looked more closely. Some of the commissioned and non-commissioned officers were familiar to me. This cannot be real, I thought. The war was over. I am in Germany not the Antarctic. I dashed into the nearest hut to recover from the shock and collect my thoughts. Fortunately, I discovered men in British Army uniform looking rather perplexed at me as I seemed to be the odd one out in this 'spiel'.

'For heaven's sake explain what is going on,' I appealed to someone standing nearby and watching.

He seemed amused. 'Are you sure you don't know? Has no one explained?'

'Know what?' I enquired, expressing ignorance. Has the war, by some stretch of the imagination restarted?'

'Of course not.'

Sanity and reality seemed to return slowly and surely. This play was for public consumption. The cameras, the light reflectors, the shouting of 'take two, take three', revealed play-acting.

'We are filming,' a man explained, dressed in what resembled a British Army uniform.

'Filming what?' I asked.

He appeared to be a very nice chap and started to explain: 'We are doing a film called *The Captive Heart* with all English actors.' He then pointed to some men dressed in shoddy and dilapidated army uniforms and continued: 'There is Michael Redgrave and standing next to him is Basil Redford and Melvyn Johns. The gentleman over there pointing to the very much better-dressed and relatively normal-looking man is Cavalcanti directing the show.'

He smiled at me and I apologised, saying that it was my first day in what appeared to be a weird and deranged place. I had not been briefed properly. All the while, my mind was working overtime: this was my chance to become an actor. In a flash, my future seemed solved. Do it gradually, I thought, by offering my services first as an interpreter and then requesting a small speaking part, preferably as a German officer. This was fame at last for me!

With no compunction or nerves, I approached Cavalcanti. 'Are you looking for German speakers?' I asked him.

'Yes, of course,' he replied.

'I'm bilingual in German and English.'

He seemed pleased and replied: 'Wonderful! We need fluent German speakers. What is your acting experience?'

'None,' I answered but added that I was very willing to learn. On reflection it was a slip-up to have given an honest reply. To bluff would have been the best thing to do in the circumstances. He laughed and explained politely that trained professional actors only were required. However, there was room for me in the non-speaking crowd scenes.

He suggested that I approach the relevant person in charge. No time was lost; I got myself enlisted and walked scantily dressed with many others across a field by the parameter of the camp. At the *Urauffuehrung* (the world premiere), in the first showing of the unabridged version of the film in cinemas, I saw an image of myself walking with others. I should have made copies and preserved them for posterity, but technology so common nowadays was not available then. Also, to my dismay, this scene was cut from later showings. Whenever there has been a repeat performance of the film I have watched the scene attentively in the hope that the status quo has been restored. No such luck so far. However, before public release back in 1946, I did have the opportunity to attend the screening of a number of scenes in the film and was immortalised in a photo printed in the *Picture Post*. It depicted a genuine German major, the equivalent English actor who played him and between them none other than myself. Fame of some sort at last.

Back to reality and mundane things, a corporal showed me round the unoccupied skeleton of the camp and led me to a small, skimpy office. He withdrew a file from the shelf; it contained a photo of two men. One was a private and the other the German equivalent of a sergeant. Certainly the higher-ranked man looked familiar. Viewing it closely, I asked: 'What is this photo doing here and why the file?'

There followed an extraordinary explanation: the British Government imposed automatic arrest for Germans who held this rank in the Nazi Party, and auxiliary services of Ortsgruppenleiter and above. These arrest categories were extended to certain select units of the German forces such as the Abwehr (counter-intelligence). Anyone who held the rank of sergeant and above was automatically arrested and held in a secure, guarded internment camp. Shortly after the end of the war, two members of the Abwehr, an ordinary private and a *Feldwebel* (Sergeant) were detained and brought to Westertimke. These were the two men featured in the photograph that had just been shown to me. The Sergeant stated his name to be Heinrich Hintzinger. The private seemed to hold his friend with excessive deference, not customary between a common soldier and a non-commissioned officer, who also wore an odd eye-patch over his right eye.

The pair looked and acted strange and inevitably drew attention to themselves, so further military help was sought. An officer was brought in and a decision taken to transfer them to Luneburg to a more specialised interrogation centre. There the sergeant was asked to remove his eye-patch and it became very clear that Hintzinger was none other than Heinrich Himmler, Hitler's right-hand man. Once discovered, and during further questioning, he swallowed a vial of poison believed to have been cyanide and died.

My time at Westertimke was an interesting one, full of unexpected contacts. Berlin had been excessively bombed by the Western and Eastern forces and its fate was still undecided, so Hamburg became the cultural centre of the British Zone. A friend with whom I shared rooms prior to and during the interpreters' school days in Brussels controlled the output of the North-West German Rundfunk (broadcasting institution), censored all artists appearing and ensured that all employees had no association, even remotely, with the old regime. Anyone with membership of Nazi organisations was banned for the time being. In my opinion he had the prime job; the most interesting, challenging, lucrative and promising, so I thought at the time. By just mentioning some of the legendary composers and artists such as Sigmund Romberg, Kurt Weil and Max Steiner who were contracted to appear made me exceedingly envious. My connection with this friend gave me an entrée to a variety of concerts. We marched in without prior warning, commanded the best possible seats and behaved as if we owned the place. He sat down with a stop watch and after each performance he met the artists and arranged meetings to discuss dates, times and venues for their next appearances. Moving from Westertimke brought these cultural exploits to an end.

Being in the vicinity of Hamburg also provided an opportunity for me to meet friends who had been with me in Gwrych Castle in Wales and who were now serving in the British Army in Germany. From one friend I heard of the exploits of Wolfgang Billig, now known as Bingham. I learned that he was a hero. He had driven an ambulance behind enemy lines despite extreme danger and rescued severely wounded Allied soldiers. For this act of heroism he was awarded the Military Medal (MM). During a visit to the services club at the Rathaus in Hamburg I bumped into him. We celebrated our 'reunion' by drinking Armagnac in true army style, something which was not in my usual small repertoire of drinks.

Bingham disappeared as quickly as he had appeared and did not re-emerge for decades after the war when I spotted him as a reporter for some obscure paper at the Jewish Ex-servicemen's Parade in Whitehall.

He was married, had lived in South Africa, then in the UK and worked as a journalist and photographer. Quite in character he then vanished, but I saw him again in November 2003 at a Jewish memorial service at the Cenotaph in London.

The camp at Westertimke, after rendering useful service to the film studios, was dismantled, but I disappeared well before the apparently exciting and memorable party given for the actors, staff and helpers. Someone who attended gave me a full report of the lavish food served (not forgetting everything was still rationed), including free drinks which I did not really miss.

My next posting was to Fallingbostel, and what happened here became the most extraordinary part of my whole army career and it had to do with interrogations and top-secret intelligence work.

The roads around Fallingbostel were relatively empty, mostly used by army personnel, doctors, ambulances or others engaged in vital services. The railway system was somewhat functioning but with problems. Limited trains were running and not always on time. The stations and trains were dangerously crowded. Fortunately at the time I had very limited experience of travelling by public transport.

On one occasion, on the way to Fallingbostel, my chauffeur-driven car broke down and I found myself stranded. Anxious to return to my living quarters as quickly as possible, and not wanting to wait for collection, I found my way amazingly easily through crowds of hustling and bustling people to the platform in Celle. My lady driver remained dutifully with the car. At the time, respect was still paid to the British uniform, though not always to a soldier's belongings.

The station master approached and asked whether he could help. I explained briefly my predicament and was advised to go to the front of the platform and listen carefully to the announcement. I did as instructed. Just as the train appeared there was a call on the tannoy. In a booming tone it announced: 'The next train arriving on platform two will call at ...' followed by a long list of stations including Fallingbostel. It continued: 'Please note the first carriage is reserved for war disabled, the severely handicapped, the blind, pregnant women and the Englishman.' I felt honoured and flushed with pride. I appeared to be in good company and my train journey was relatively uneventful. To start with I may have inhibited free-and-easy conversation; there was still a feeling of fear of authority which I seemed to evoke by my uniform. This relaxed when I spoke to some of them in polite Hochdeutsch followed by an offer of English cigarettes more valuable than any currency. This broke the ice. The not uncommon repertoire of hardship followed. It sounded as if they expected an apology from me for starting the war. But I relaxed when they eventually exonerated the British, either for political or most likely for 'commercial' reasons, from all the evils afflicting the West Germans currently. Was it the cigarettes, or politeness? Perhaps a bit of both.

Fallingbostal was not *klein kleckersdorf* but a moderately-sized, prosperous, clean-looking residential town not far from the Lüneburg Heath. The intelligence section occupied an impressive and spacious house in the best part of town. I parked my Matchless 350 motorbike at the side entrance, carried my sparse amount of luggage to the first floor, unpacked and waited to meet my commanding officer. The door opened and a medium-built officer walked in and introduced himself as Captain Rollo Reid.

'You're Rothman, I presume', he said.

My immediate impression was that here was a man I could get on with without difficulty. He did not brief me but invited me to have a cup of tea. We went to the dining room and sat down, and a middle-aged woman appeared and explained in German that she was the cook and general bottle-washer. She vanished, returning a few minutes later carrying a tray with a fine china teapot, cups and saucers, silver spoons and, to my amazement, homemade *kirschentorte* (cherry gateaux). For the moment I thought I had left this world and entered heaven. Rollo Reid proceeded to explain that the offices were several kilometres away and he would brief me the next morning. Meanwhile, he told me: 'Make yourself comfortable and we'll meet this evening for a drink when I will introduce you to the other fellows.'

Evening came and to my utter surprise and delight at the dining-room table sat Henry Howard Marcel Roberts, Peter Blake (formerly Blau) and Ralph Parker – my fellow students from the interpreters' school in Brussels. They had arrived earlier in the day. Together we formed part of the 3rd Counter-Intelligence Section. In the army I was known as Harry Rothman (Hermann Rothman).

We were joined a little later by Ernest Alastair Gordon MacGarrety (formerly Rummelsburg). He was the son of Dr Rummelsburg, a medical practitioner then living in Southend-on-Sea in Essex. Together with Captain Reid we formed a very closely-knit group devoted to what we believed to be a worthwhile cause. We enjoyed each other's company outside our working hours. Apart from MacGarrety, the rest of the group were slightly older and more experienced than me. Roberts (that's how we addressed him) had served in No. 10 Inter-Allied Commando and had trained with other German-speaking refugees in 3 Troop. Peter Blake was tall and good-looking; an imposing figure who shared rooms with me. We became particularly good friends. Parker (which is how he was always known), the son of a German lawyer, was a slight young man with fair hair and a blonde moustache; consciously or unconsciously he emulated his father, wagging his finger when giving us the legal position on any subject under discussion – English or German. MacGarrety (Mac) was the bohemian member of our team – public schoolboy, soprano saxophone player with a pronounced upper-class accent. Having the advantage of living in England for a longer period than the rest of us, he had acquired exaggerated English habits both in speech and behaviour. He considered me a fellow musician. Exceptionally good-hearted, we too became great friends. Unfortunately, Mac was called back to England on compassionate leave. His younger brother had been killed when a ball had hit him during a cricket match at school. It was some weeks before Mac returned to the team.

The five of us shared a similar background: all were born in Germany, were bilingual and Jewish, however, the Jewishness of most of the others was remote. Their impression of our commanding officer, Captain Reid, confirmed mine: mainly easy-going, obliging, helpful, plus other engaging qualities, and above all, he presented a totally different experience from my earlier primary training. Remarkable harmony prevailed between all the members of the section, common objectives closely cementing us. Rolo Reid's knowledge of German was 'school German', whereas the rest of us were bilingual; our life experience not only reflected our characters but also our expressions in linguistic terms. This was appreciated and respected by him. During the days that followed I discovered that Rollo Reid had studied accountancy before joining the army and that on his demob he intended to become a chartered accountant.

The morning after our arrival, we jumped in the jeep and drove to our offices which adjoined the internment camp. They were in a pleasant building attached to a former POW camp for Allied soldiers which had been liberated by British troops in mid-April 1945. Fallingbostel camp was also known as Stalag 11B and had contained 6,500 British and American prisoners, and another called Stalag 357 with some 3,500 POWs. Some of the Allied prisoners had been there for nearly a year since the difficult campaign around Villers-Bocage in France in June and July 1944. By the time we were there it housed all German Nazi POWs who came within the British Army arrest categories, possibly wanted for war crimes, for example, members of the NSDAP and the Ortsgruppenleiter (Senior District Party Officials).

British Intelligence had the bright idea of combing through the local telephone directory which proudly displayed the rank of all Nazi officials. They were subsequently telephoned and invited to a meeting where we promptly arrested them. However, some were unable to attend and sent a relative in their place or an official of lower rank to represent them. This caused immense problems of how to sort out the real villains from the bystanders. It was not merely a matter of trust; those in question needed thorough investigation, often involving detailed and lengthy searches. Anyone could claim not to be a named official and escape the net, or could abscond after being informed of our unique method of arrest. Often high-ranking Nazi officials, even those suspected of war crimes, declared themselves 'unable' to attend these meetings for various reasons (legitimate or otherwise) and escaped. But eventually, relatively few escaped the Allies, and those that did fled to a haven in South America.

Fallingbostal was a large camp. The detainees were separated into different arrest categories and split into five compounds A–E. In E Compound, high-ranking officers, potential war criminals and Nazi officials from *Kreisleiter* upwards were incarcerated. There was also a women's section consisting of high- and low-ranking Nazis, auxiliary organisations as well as Gestapo members. A major was in charge of the camp but our section was independent. The prisoners were interrogated and then categorised. Those who were regarded as suspected war criminals were transferred to a specialised camp. Similarly, high-ranking military officers were eventually separated for further, more detailed interrogation. Some were discharged if it was felt they had been wrongly arrested.

Our captain, Rollo Reid, suggested a regular daily routine for us to follow. Before the morning interrogation got under way we had a short meeting for approximately fifteen minutes. We then prepared a list of people whom we wished to question. This was followed by dictating reports to our German staff. A problem then arose about which of our German typists could be trusted with confidential or secret information. So they had to be interrogated first and their trustworthiness ascertained. Unfortunately, the time available was too short to conduct a full investigation into their suitability and so we used our judgement, but over time we were proved right in our intuitive conclusions about them.

The time schedule had to be adhered to for a number of reasons. Our secretaries had to start and finish on time; the office and papers cleared and locked up. Any exchange of interesting or comic episodes was reserved for the evening table, as were other matters which needed joint discussion and attention among the intelligence staff.

One evening we had a rather frightening episode. Two privates attached to our section served as drivers and general factotum. They were totally different in character from each other: one being rather dull and obedient; the other articulate, non-conforming and at times obstinate and questioning of orders. The reason for his odd behaviour came to light at a later stage. He came from a middle-class home and should have received promotion, possibly becoming an officer, but had suffered a nervous breakdown. As a result, he had been reduced to doing menial tasks. The following episode brought to light his psycho-pathological state of mind. During the mealtime, as we were seated around the table, he burst into the room brandishing his rifle and threatened to kill us. Stunned into total silence, we failed to respond. After a lengthy pause, one of us, who considered himself somewhat of a psychologist (namely myself), quietly stood up and invited him to come outside. Surprisingly he responded. Thinking the matter at an end and feeling triumphant, I asked him to give me the rifle. But he replied: 'No! Not before I've shot someone.' He began randomly shooting into the air and taking steps back into the house. Trying to calm him down by speaking to him again, sanity eventually prevailed and he handed me his rifle. Needless to say, steps were taken to have him posted away as quickly as possible.

Our work at Fallingbostel was never dull. One day the alarm bells sounded and we were summoned to a general meeting. We were told to expect an intake of 160 detainees from Norway. To our utter surprise they were all women between the ages of twenty and thirty and were all German. None of them looked impoverished. They were well-dressed, attractive and well-fed; their hair beautifully arranged. The war seemed to have passed them by. In a way we were shocked. In France, Belgium and Holland, and even Germany, we had seen women of similar age suffering starvation, wearing rags, with their hair all dishevelled. Then we remembered why we were there and why they stood as our prisoners.

Our German clerical staff took down administrative details followed by our interrogation. An extraordinary story unfolded. The party of women consisted of conscripts and volunteers. We questioned what they were doing in Norway. What was their function? Some answers were very obvious. Some were women of easy virtue. Some were the equivalent of ENSA (entertainment) and others simply performed administrative duties. Others had been asked to perpetuate the Nordic and Aryan race. The problem for us was how to differentiate and classify this group. To interrogate them was no problem. They were very cooperative and spoke freely. At our dinner table discussion, our group considered the dilemma. The consensus of opinion was that only a minority did not like their allotted tasks. One must not forget that German success between 1939 and 1943 inculcated and confirmed the belief of the *Herrenvolk* idea, i.e. being superior and better than any other race. Consequently, their actions in occupied territories confirmed this belief.

The influx of these ladies into the camp caused unexpected problems. A report was found on our desk stating that the barbed wire separating the female internees had been cut and permission was sought to question the persons responsible. We had no objections to the request, but wanted to know the results of the investigation. Shocked to learn that it was not just one individual but a group, we exercised understanding and wisdom and took no further action, except to recommend the strengthening of the barbed wire on all fencing. To everyone's amusement they were then reduced to shouting loud and clear, private and confidential words of endearment. Those women who needed further investigation were eventually transferred to another camp. The majority were freed and some carried out clerical work in our office.

On another occasion, the military police brought into the camp a high-ranking German officer who had been found hiding in a small village in the Lüneburg Heath. He had foolishly not discarded his uniform but appeared fully outfitted as a German general, clad in all his military regalia. I was asked to conduct a very short preliminary interrogation. When I approached him and asked him for his name, rank and number he gave it freely. But when I started asking him further questions he laid down one condition: 'I want to be interrogated only by a man of my rank.' As he was a general it was difficult to find a German-speaking British general in the camp. I explained the difficulties but came up with a solution. I reduced him to the rank of private by removing his insignia, epaulettes and other signs of rank, and then asked him whether I as a sergeant, and his superior, could carry out the interrogation. However, I added that I would try to find a German-speaking private and his conditions for speaking freely would then be fully complied with. He could see from this that the British Army, in contrast to the German military, was very accommodating. He was rendered completely speechless by my approach. Later that day I told my colleagues at dinner and hilarious laughter resulted from my quick-witted response to the situation that had faced me.

One particular morning Captain Reid came into my office with a request that I act as an observer. A little later he explained that a German defence lawyer by the name of Dr Servatius would be calling by to meet a selected number of high-ranking internees in preparation for a forth-coming trial. Reid gave me a prepared list of just over a dozen names, all of whom Dr Servatius wished to interview. On the list was Gauleiter Forster, the infamous Gauleiter of Danzig, who had committed many atrocities in his region, plus a number of German generals and former high-ranking government officials. Shortly afterwards, the attorney arrived at my office and we made our way to the conference room. It was a grey, dull-looking room with one window. When we entered it the internees were already assembled. Their faces portrayed a question-ing expression − what is in store for us? Dr Servatius introduced himself and explained that at the forthcoming hearing he would represent some of those present and, in particular, Gauleiter Forster. He then posed a number of questions to Forster, all relating to the Danzig area for which Forster had overall responsibility. Servatius explained the allegations, namely that in Forster's region there had been mass executions without trial. Forster emphatically denied this. Listening to the questions and answers, I got the impression that Forster was a minor executive, who ministered his region as a benign and compassionate Burgermeister, completely in accordance with democratic law and order. But I was wrong. And this view was not shared by an elderly German general present, who jumped up from the table and began shouting at Forster.

Of course, I understood every word he said. 'Sie Luegner!' (You liar!), he shouted. He went on to say that there had been mass executions in Danzig and on every tree along the main road people were hanging without trial because they were racially and politically unacceptable. Dr Servatius in a calm and dignified way responded to the general, telling him that there would be opportunities to hear his version of what took place in Danzig at a later stage. This had an effect on Forster and his benevolent description of what took place in this area. Not only did his demeanour change but he became very careful of his utterances. Until that moment, his replies had been long party speeches. What now followed were short, curt sentences, often just 'yes' or 'no'.

I reflected on the general's outburst and interpreted it as follows: he had entered the German *Heer* (army) as a young man in the early 1920s. At that point Germany was a democratic country, within limits, and its democratic flavour drifted through to the forces. One was able to express opinions unrestricted but still had to adhere to the discipline of army life. Hitler's army, on the other hand, was 'Ja! Oder Nein! Mein Führer!' Most were able to adapt, some temporarily, but others (just a very small number) could never really adjust. They simply said 'Goodbye mein Führer!' This general I would put in the grey category. However, it would seem that after defeat he turned. It is possible that all his emotions, bottled up for many years, suddenly exploded in front of us. My later conversations with him confirmed that view. His outburst and my presence must have had a restraining effect on the others present as many were silent. This may also be attributed to the many years when free expression was forbidden.

I found Dr Servatius a man of few words. He seemed to instil an element of trust in the internees. All questions posed by him were direct and to the point. He abstained from expressing opinions, moralising or saying anything which would impede a free flow of expression. I met him on several other occasions and could fully understand why this gifted man was later given the difficult job of defending the arch-criminal Adolf Eichmann.

From time to time permission was sought by other intelligence units to interrogate individuals who were held in our camp. A date and time were fixed and rooms were made available for this purpose. One such person who arrived to interrogate prisoners was Robert Maxwell (original name Abraham Lajbi Hoch from a Czech village), later a businessman, publishing and newspaper tycoon. At that time he was an intelligence officer whose courage as a soldier was well known amongst personnel and soldiers in the British forces. He had joined the North Staffordshire Regiment in 1943, was proficient in several European languages and so was recruited into the intelligence section. In 1944 he landed with his regiment in Normandy as a sniper sergeant. After participating in the hard-fought battle for the Orne bridgehead, he was commissioned in the field as a second lieutenant. In 1945 he was awarded a Military Cross by Field Marshal Montgomery and promoted to the rank of captain for single-handedly attacking German machine gunners who were obstructing the advance of his regiment. Maxwell came to our camp with an assistant and furnished us with a brief, giving details of why he wished to interview one particular internee. At that time Maxwell created a very favourable impression on our team. Little did we know then that many years later he would receive notoriety, and in 1991 he died in mysterious circumstances, having disappeared from his yacht *Lady Ghislaine*. His body was recovered from the sea somewhere off the Canary Islands.

On a pleasantly warm day that summer, while going through A Compound, I saw someone seated in front of an easel painting the landscape. This section contained *mitlaufers* (fellow travellers). I quite openly admired his work and spent some time discussing art and, in particular, landscape in oil and watercolour. He showed me quite a number of his paintings and added that anyone who has an artistic flair could paint reasonably well. I admitted that although I did not consider myself an artist, I sometimes had the desire to put brush to canvas. He responded in a friendly way and expressed his willingness to teach me the rudiments of landscape painting. Shortly afterwards I went on leave and returned to the camp equipped with artists materials and full of enthusiasm. He taught me a great deal and in a short time I came to grips with the rudiments. I was indeed surprised by the end product. Many years later, not surprisingly, I studied one year's modernism at the Open University and my vista widened considerably, to such an extent that in retirement I now spend many happy hours at the Tate and Tate Modern as well as The Royal Academy.

What a contrast between our German POWs in Fallingbostel and the Allied POWs incarcerated by the Germans? For the Allied POWs there was a reasonably quick release after the war. But for the German POWs held in camps run by the Allies, especially those in our camp, there was total uncertainty about the future.

It was during July 1945 that someone suggested to us that we invite survivors of Bergen-Belsen concentration camp for lunch. The former concentration camp was situated not far from us but, in spite of being liberated back in April, it still had many thousands of survivors in it. Some lived at the former barracks; many were patients at nearby hospitals and, unfortunately, many were still dying. The death toll rose almost daily. We contacted the administrators of the camp and a date was set and arrangements made for a group to visit us for a meal. A day or so before, a somewhat heated discussion took place concerning the format. Eventually we all agreed to play it by ear but under no circumstances should the word KZ (concentration camp) be mentioned or any reference made to their confinement. The dietary requirements followed; we made sure we prepared a vegetarian and also a fish meal. We then arranged for two cars to collect them. It would turn out to be an extraordinary meal, one which has left a lasting impression on me. It still touches me deeply today when I think of it, and reduces me to weeping. The day of the lunch arrived; the seating had been arranged and the guests arrived punctually. To our complete surprise, all were teenage girls. Not particularly tall, nicely dressed and understandably they looked apprehensive, as did we. At the start, conversation was difficult so this enabled us to eat the meal.

The lunch appeared to be finished when, to our great surprise, they mentioned Hungary, their life with their parents and what led to their arrest. What followed astonished us and saddened us greatly. Towards the latter part of 1944 Jews were ordered to assemble in a large field – many thousands of Jews of all ages and sexes surrounded by Hungarian Army soldiers who, without empathy, sorted them out into the young, middle-aged, seniors and the very old. Leaving behind parents and relatives, the large group to which our young guests belonged were marched away, guarded by the Hungarians. Their destination remained unknown for a while. They crossed the border into Slovakia and still the final destination was not apparent; a few lagged behind, unable to keep pace with the large group. Food supply became short. Marched through towns and villages, they appealed for food and water but to no avail. Shutters were closed and curtains drawn. Only on a few occasions would a very brave person respond by providing bread for them. The callousness of the indigenous populations reflected an underlying bitterness towards our young guests. At times during their march, weather conditions were appalling; their clothes, worn and tattered, gave little protection. They felt totally betrayed. Their numbers greatly depleted, they arrived at Bergen-Belsen concentration camp. This nightmare journey left them with an indelible imprint. It was a shock to us to hear their story.

With our lunch finally over, they bade their farewells to us and expressed the wish to reciprocate by inviting us to lunch at their barracks in Belsen, to which we agreed. The date was fixed and we arrived at the barracks in Belsen laden with our gifts of tea, coffee and chocolates. We walked up two flights of stairs, knocked at the door and were greeted with a surprise. A very large but sparsely furnished room contained a number of trestle tables covered with white tablecloths. The tables, decorated with wild flowers placed in clean jars, astonished and delighted us. However simple the scene was, it created such an impression on me and I was unable to suppress my tears. As it is customary amongst ortho-dox observant Jewish people, we were invited to wash our hands, say the blessing over the bread and sit down at the table. Despite the fact that some of us had for many years not experienced this ritual, we neverthe-less all responded and gave the impression that it was part of our life so as not to embarrass our hosts. Despite the sparse meal, we could see that these young girls had made a great effort. It could be seen in their faces and their demeanours. There was a jolly atmosphere with laughter and jokes, in contrast to their visit to us. The thought occurred to me then that these young girls, who had endured untenable barbaric hardships, maintained their dignity, retained their faith and did not shrug off the civilised lessons of their parents even under such difficult circumstances.

6

Hitler's Will

Our small group of interrogators at Fallingbostel, all German refugees in British Army uniform, established a very disciplined routine. We got up at a certain time, had breakfast and left for the office at 8.30 a.m. We stopped for lunch at the house at one o'clock, had a little conference and resumed work at 2 p.m. We always endeavoured to be back at the house at 6 p.m. in time for dinner. It sounds very Teutonic but it was in perfect keeping with our original Germanic background. The evenings were also well organised. Understandably, we were conscientious, well-disciplined, supportive, argumentative and loyal to each other. In a few words we were 'comrades in arms'.

Given our strict adherence to routine, it came as a huge shock when the telephone rang at 5 a.m. one autumn morning. We were all naturally fast asleep. I thought it was part of my dream, but the telephone continued to ring. Then I realised it was no dream but something of importance. I picked it up and heard Rollo Reid say, 'Please come to the office immediately. I will explain then.' To say it sounded strange would be an understatement. My mind was racing as I quickly dressed, had a coffee and dashed to the office. We all assembled before Reid. There was Henry Howard Marcel Roberts, Peter Blake, Ralph Parker, Ernest Alastair Gorden MacGarrety and me. Reid immediately ordered one of us to lock the door. Everything appeared to be odd. What could be so important for all of us to be summoned to one room and the door locked?

In order to understand what followed, it is important to briefly explain the work of the camp administration unit. Shortly before the war had finished, the arrest categories were formulated into 'Arrest' or 'Suspected of War Crimes'. Germans who fell within certain categories were arrested and brought to camps like Fallingbostel, where they were immediately searched by army personnel for any items or material of intelligence value. Depending on what was found on the prisoners, some items were destroyed, some retained and others given back after their arrest. The head of this search unit was a corporal who had been a display manager in civilian life at the London West End branch of Aquascutum. His assistant was a lance corporal who had also previously been in the clothing business. Both, therefore, had a keen eye for discovering anything irregular or abnormal while searching new internees. It was extraordinary what 'smoking gun' material some internees carried with them. For example, some carried letters of praise from the Führer and other high-ranking Nazis, which they used as references. In one particular instance, while interrogating a *Kreisleiter* who denied he was an ardent Nazi supporter, I asked him to explain why he had a letter of recommendation from his gauleiter. I then read to him the relevant passages. He explained that in his heart he was opposed to the regime but had these papers as his *Sicherheitsgarantie* (security guarantee).

Back to the incident in question: the corporal had been informed that during the night a man was apprehended while crossing the Russian/British Zone border of Berlin and then transferred to our internment camp. During the routine search, the corporal had noticed the unusual bulkiness of the man's shoulder pads. He asked him to remove his jacket. The corporal then proceeded to rip open the shoulders and found a number of pages of parchment typed in capital letters. He instantly recognised that these must be documents of importance, even though they were typed in German and he could not understand them. Seeking advice he put them in a safe place and telephoned Captain Reid. Surprised by the phone call during the middle of the night, Rollo Reid at first questioned being woken up. What could be so urgent? The corporal then gave him a brief description of the find and Reid realised the significance of the documents, which warranted further, immediate investigation. When arriving at the office Rollo Reid discovered that the signature shown to him on some of the parchments appeared to be that of Adolf Hitler. Reid now needed urgent confirmation and telephoned us, the German-speaking refugees, immediately. This was the explanation for having woken us at such an unearthly hour.

The man on whom the parchment had been found was Heinz Lorenz. During his interrogation, the story unfolded: By 25 April 1945 the Russian army had completely surrounded Berlin and access to the capital remained possible only by air. Delivery of news came through the Press Officer who was Heinz Lorenz. It was Heinz Lorenz who brought to Adolf Hitler's bunker the dramatic information of Himmler's betrayal, quoting a British Reuters report. Lorenz added that Himmler was in negotiation with Count Bernadotte, who during the war had been negotiating the release of Jews in the camps in exchange for German POWs. Lorenz gave a copy of the Reuters report directly to Hitler's secretary, Martin Bormann, and Joseph Goebbels, the propaganda minister. During later British interrogations of Lorenz, he confirmed that before news items were presented to Hitler they had to be censored by Goebbels. After a further meeting with Goebbels, Lorenz was urged to go and meet with Martin Bormann. Before he left on his mission, he said goodbye to Hitler who remained silent and just shook his hand. Not surprisingly, Lorenz saw that the Führer looked sombre and dishevelled, with prominent bags under his eyes. Little did Lorenz know then that it would be the last time he saw the Führer.

On 30 April 1945 Adolf Hitler and his newly-wed mistress Eva Braun committed suicide in the underground bunker. In taking his own life, Hitler had ensured that the Allied powers could not bring him to justice. At the time of Hitler's suicide, Lorenz had already left for his meeting with Martin Bormann. At that meeting Lorenz was handed Hitler's personal and political Will by Bormann. Afterwards, Lorenz contacted Joseph Goebbels who entrusted him with his own addendum to Hitler's Will. The Wills and the addendum are reproduced in appendices to this book. The top-secret British intelligence report compiled after the interrogation of Lorenz has now been declassified at the Public Record Office, Kew. It makes interesting reading:

Hitler's will has been discovered. It was found on Heinz Lorenz, INB journalist who had been attached to Hitler's staff since 1936. Before the war Lorenz attended a number of important conferences between Hitler and Foreign Statesmen and recorded the proceedings in shorthand. During the war he was attached to the Führer's headquarters and took down news received from foreign broadcasts and passed it direct to the Führer's Staff. In this capacity he was working at the bunker in the Reichchancellery from 18th April '45 onwards, his receiving set acting as the only link between the outside world and the Führer's bunker (he was unable to transmit messages). It was he who broke Hitler the news of Mussolini's death and also of Himmler's negotiations with Count Bernadotte. He [Lorenz] was arrested in the British Zone, where he was living under an alias, taken to an internment camp and there searched. Sewn into the shoulder padding of his coat were found the following documents:

Hitler's Personal Will
Hitler's Personal Testament
An Appendix by Goebbels to Hitler's Political Testament

He has been interrogated in detail on how he came into possession of these documents and he has given a story of the last days in Hitler's bunker which agrees practically in every detail with that already given to the Press on 1st November. As he was so frequently in the bunker he was in contact with Hitler's adjutants and members of his Staff and was able to obtain a very good idea of what was going on. He says that it was the news of Himmler's negotiations which made Hitler finally decide to marry Eva Braun and commit suicide. At 0400 hrs, on 29th April Hitler made his wills, which were witnessed by Bormann, Goebbels, Gen. Krebs (Chief of the General Staff), Gen. Burgdorf and Col. Von Below (Luftwaffe Adjutant at Führer HQ.)

Between 0900 and 1000 hrs on the same morning, Lorenz was summoned by Bormann who gave him Hitler's personal and political wills. He was then given Goebbels' declaration by Goebbels himself. He was instructed to leave Berlin at once in civilian clothes and convey the wills to [Admiral] Doenitz if possible, or failing him, the nearest German High Command. He was told by Goebbels that if all else failed, he was to publish the wills for historical purposes. Bormann told Lorenz that he had been given this mission because as a young man with plenty of initiative, it was considered that he had a good chance of getting through. Lorenz left Berlin on 29th April at midday and was subsequently not present at the time of Hitler's suicide. As he found it impossible to reach Doenitz he decided to attempt to live under a cover name and to await events.

Lorenz's story has been checked against all available evidence and appears to be entirely reliable. The signatures on the documents have been compared with other signatures of Hitler, Bormann and Goebbels and pronounced by an expert to be genuine. They have also been shown to Otto Dietrich, Hitler's Press Chief, and were immediately recognised by him. The wills bear out the evidence we have from other sources that Hitler intended to commit suicide and have his body burnt together with that of Eva Braun. He definitely states this intention in his personal will, in which he leaves all his possessions to the Party (or the State if the Party no longer exists), except for his paintings which are to be used for the foundation of a picture gallery at Linz, and any personal mementos which his family or his former Secretaries might wish to keep.

His political testament is divided into two parts, the first being a tirade disclaiming all responsibility for the war and blaming it on the Jews, who he says were the real agency which led England into war in 1939. In this he again states that he has no intention of falling into enemy hands, but will instead stay in Berlin and choose death voluntarily at the moment when he feels his position can no longer be maintained. He orders, however, the rest of the German people to continue fighting with all possible means.

More information about Lorenz came to light during his interrogation at our unit than given in the report above. Lorenz described how on 30 April 1945 he dressed in civilian clothes, together with Willi Johannmeier, Wilhelm Zander and Hummerich, and left for the Pfaueninsel (an island in the Havel river, running through the suburbs of Berlin). They hoped that Admiral Doenitz would provide them with a plane so that they could leave the encircled capital before complete Russian occupation. No plane arrived, and avoiding the heavy Soviet artillery fire, they procured a canoe; then on finding a small yacht they used it as a temporary shelter. In the pitch darkness and in the roaring bombardment they heard the droning of a plane which they assumed Admiral Doenitz had sent for them.

They saw the shadow of an aircraft alight on the water and Lorenz and Zander made their way towards it. Johannmeier remained on the yacht, using his torch to draw the attention of the pilot. On reaching the plane and while speaking to the pilot, Zander overturned his boat. Immediately his companions tried to rescue him but were hindered by the Russians intensive firing at the plane. The pilot suddenly took fright and flew off. He subsequently lied, reporting to Admiral Doenitz that he had tried desperately to find the four men but had failed, and regrettably he had had to abandon the search.

The men left behind now started a remarkable journey through the perimeter of the River Havel, first to the Pfaueninsel, back to the yacht, and then to the deserted Wannsee, a popular bathing resort with Berliners. They managed to find their way to Potsdam and Brandenburg. Before crossing the River Elbe, Lorenz suggested that the others should get rid of their uniforms. They did and found plenty of civilian clothes left by fleeing foreign labourers. It proved an excellent disguise. They made their farewells and parted company, at least for the foreseeable future. Lorenz paired up with Zander.

There were three Russian checkpoints in Berlin to be negotiated before entering the less difficult parts of the suburbs. There was chaos. People were desperately trying to leave the warzone in Berlin and, therefore, Lorenz and Zander were impeded in their plans to make contact with Admiral Doenitz. They then decided to split up and make their own way. Through great adversity Lorenz eventually ended up in Luxembourg and found work as a journalist under the assumed name of George Thiers.

With the war over and things returning somewhat to normal, Lorenz thought the time was ripe to disclose that he had information of great interest. He approached the British authorities in Hanover for work and offered to give details of life inside Hitler's bunker. Questions were asked as to how he had acquired this knowledge. As his answers were not clearly expressed, suspicions were aroused and he was subsequently arrested. This was how he was brought to Fallingbostel.

During interrogation he admitted that his real name was Heinz Lorenz, and that he had been Goebbels' Press Attaché. Through the professionalism of our Corporal, the very important historical documents of Hitler's Will were discovered. Lorenz was then interrogated in great detail. A man in his early thirties, he spoke freely, and our joint assessment of him at the time was that he was a *Mitlaeufer* (someone who ran with the pack). In other words, he was a shrewd man who was motivated entirely by self-interest. We were given strict orders that the arrest of Lorenz should in no way be discussed outside our section and above all it should not be leaked to the press. A search was made for the other two couriers. The first to be discovered was Zander in the American Zone.

Although Zander's home was in Munich, evidence showed that he had not visited his home since the end of the war. His wife lived with her parents in Hanover and claimed not to have seen her husband since the war had finished. She freely provided photographs of him and gave the addresses of his mother and brothers. Frau Zander stated that her husband was no longer alive and this was the belief also of his parents. Further enquiries were made. It was discovered that he was in fact living under the false name of Friedrich-Wilhelm Paustin and working as a market gardener in Bavaria. With the help of the American Counter-Intelligence Corps he was found at the home of Martin Bormann's secretary in the little village of Aidenbach near Passau on the Austrian border. During interrogation Zander confirmed Lorenz's story. He confessed to having been an ardent Nazi but, in common with most of his fellow travellers, now saw the 'light'. It is true, he said, that the documents were in Hanover but, as it was impossible to deliver them to Admiral Doenitz, they were brought to Munich and concealed in a suit-case at the property of friends. Without difficulties, a copy of Hitler's two testaments were retrieved, together with his marriage certificate. Zander confirmed that the third copy was with Johannmeier.

Going back to the early hours of that unforgettable morning, Captain Rollo Reid proceeded to distribute the parchments amongst us. He asked whether we could identify what we held in our hands. This was the first time I had seen such large impressive typed characters. Unanimously we burst out saying, 'This is Hitler's Will. Not a copy but the *original*.'

The pages changed hands; we carefully read and scrutinised the papers and confirmed earlier findings. Captain Reid then began to organise the translation amongst us. The documents of Hitler's private Will and his political Will were given to my colleagues. Goebbels' addendum to Hitler's Political Will was given to me. We retired to our offices, one man per office and were ordered to lock the door. We were not to be disturbed until we had finished our translations. This was serious, top-secret business. Once alone I felt totally isolated. There was no one to talk to and no one to consult. My office, sparsely furnished with a desk, several chairs and filing cabinets, without home comforts, produced a surreal feeling. Realising the urgency of the translation, nevertheless,

I felt momentarily handicapped by my Germanic obsession for detail which caused a break in my work. I read the addendum several times to understand what Goebbels wished to convey. My first reaction on reading it endorsed my opinion of the man — blindly loyal, a lover of words and opinionated. Goebbels camouflaged reality, equating his power base with that of Hitler. Goering and Himmler in contrast had seen the collapse of the regime as a political opportunity to rise again by discarding Hitler but not abandoning Nazi ideology.

I translated the addendum which consisted of long sentences — the specific hallmark of Goebbels; he rigidly kept to this. The opening words of the addendum were: 'In this delirium of betrayal ...' When the translation was finally filed with the official government papers, my original translation of the phrase 'in this delirium of betrayal' was changed to 'in this delirium of treason'. There is a subtle but important difference between the two and that changes the meaning. The word 'betrayal' points directly to Goering. The full translation was as follows:

The Führer has ordered me to leave Berlin if the defence of the Reich capital collapses and take part as a leading member in a government appointed by him.

For the first time in my life I must categorically refuse to obey an order of the Führer. My wife and children join me in this refusal. Otherwise, apart from the fact that on grounds of fellow feeling and personal loyalty we could never bring ourselves to leave the Führer alone in his hour of greatest need, I would appear for the rest of my life as a dishonourable traitor and common scoundrel, who would lose his own self respect as well as the respect of his fellow-citizens, a respect I should need in any further service in the future shaping of the German Nation and German State.

In the delirium of treason which surrounds the Führer in these most critical days of the war, there must be at least some people to stay with him unconditionally until death, even if this contradicts the formal, and from a material point of view, entirely justifiable order which he gives in this political testament.

I believe that I am thereby doing the best service to the future of the German people. In the hard times to come, examples will be more important than men. Men will always be found to show the nation the way out of its tribulations, but a reconstruction of our national life would be impossible if it were not developed on the basis of clear and easily understandable examples. For this reason, together with my wife, and on behalf of my children, who are too young to be able to speak for themselves, but who, if they were sufficiently old, would agree with this decision without reservation, I express my unalterable decision not to leave the Reich capital even if it falls and, at the side of the Führer to end a life which for as personally will have no further value if I cannot spend it in the service of the Führer and by his side.

Berlin 29 April 1945, 5.30 hrs
Signed: Dr Goebbels

After finishing the translations we exchanged documents and notes, carefully scrutinising each other's translation. Rollo Reid pressed us to finish the job quickly as he had somewhat prematurely contacted Lieutenant-General Brian Horrocks informing him of the find of 'some very important documents'.

Equipped with the originals and our translation, Captain Reid, Roberts, Parker, Peter Blake and I very excitedly set off for headquarters. We arrived well before noon. The guards and office staff had been forewarned of our imminent arrival and we were immediately ushered into Lt Gen Horrocks' office. A tall, slim commanding figure, accompanied by several other officers, greeted us and briefly recounted the earlier telephone conversation he had had with Rollo Reid. Before perusing the documents he dismissed his staff and spoke privately with us. He was then shown the original documents and our translation. Very briefly he questioned us and explained that his next step would be to telephone London to ascertain the genuineness of the papers. With an air of ebullience he brought out the champagne and made a short speech, complimenting us on the swift and efficient way that we had dealt with this exceptional find.

High-spirited, we returned to our office in Fallingbostel, but this feeling of euphoria did not last long. We awoke next morning to a telephone call from our commanding officer Colonel Proudlock and instead of complimenting us for all the work we had done, we got a rocket.

He bellowed: 'How dare you contact General Horrocks without speaking to me first. You have completely ignored army procedure and regulations and made me look a complete fool.'

Rollo Reid held the telephone up and asked if we could hear the commotion. We now knew that this ended our hopes of recognition and being awarded at least a medal. Captain Reid answered the colonel by inviting punishment, knowing full well that this was not possible as we had already gone to the highest authority. Until that time our dealings with the colonel had always been proper and reasonable. But this was by no means the end of the matter. Following this episode we received instructions not to divulge our find to anyone, but to exercise complete silence. It was classified as Top Secret. It left a number of questions unanswered, such as: Why had Lorenz been entrusted with the original Will of Hitler, and who had the copies? Officially we received an order not to pursue the matter anymore. But curiosity got the better of us and private enquiries had to be conducted out of business hours. On reflection, Proudlock's indignation was understandable. The army is governed by a massive number of 'do's and don'ts' and its success depends on the strictest observance of this code. In our excitement we broke the hierarchy of command and authority.

At subsequent interrogations it became apparent that the one-time obscure Heinz Lorenz had come into prominence simply because he was in the bunker shortly before Hitler's death. Being a trusted employee of Goebbels, he brought the urgent and treacherous news of Himmler's deceit and betrayal. This necessitated a complete change to the original plans. We learnt that three copies of Hitler's Political Testament and Private Will were made because delivery of the original was uncertain. One was handed to Major Willi Johannmeier (Hitler's army adjutant) to be delivered to Field Marshal Schoerner, the lately appointed commander-in-chief. Johannmeier was entrusted with the task of escorting his two comrades safely through the Russian lines and then each on to their separate destinations. Another copy of the political and personal Will was given to SS Standartenfuehrer Wilhelm Zander (Bormann's personal adviser) to be handed to Admiral Doenitz. The third, which was the original, was handed to Heinz Lorenz. Only this third one included Geobbels' personal Addendum. This was also meant to be delivered to Admiral Doenitz and from thence to Munich, the cradle of National Socialism, to be held eternally. The reason for Admiral Doenitz receiving the only copy of Goebbels' addendum to the Führer's Will has been suggested that the propaganda minister thought in terms of history. He, the person nearest to Hitler who had given him his continuous, undivided loyalty and devotion as his partner in shaping Nazi ideology with a 'new set of Ten Commandments', was the co-creator of the Third German Reich. He thought this would immortalise him. This was vanity in the extreme.

As instructed, our section kept the rule of silence to the outside world. Any discussion of what happened was confined to the small circle of translators. Reflecting on what was in the Will, we were surprised that Hitler had so little to pass on to posterity. We always imagined that he had a vast fortune. True to form, in his political Will he had much to say, of course, in blaming the Jews for Germany's misfortunes. How ironic then that a group of ex-German Jews were given the task of translating his Last Will and Testament.

A number of weeks passed and nothing further was heard. Then one morning the world woke up to the news which appeared in American papers: 'Hitler's Will has been found in the American Zone.'

We kept our promise not to divulge our find but here the Americans were claiming to have found the Will in their zone. During interrogation Lorenz gave all the information necessary to trace the other two couriers. Zander, as mentioned, was living under the false name of Friedrich-Wilhelm Paustin and was discovered in a Bavarian village in the American Zone. Once found and arrested, he talked freely and confirmed what Lorenz had said earlier. Johannmeier had found sanctuary with his parents in Iserlohn in the British Zone. In early interrogation he denied having a copy of Hitler's Will. However, the evidence against him was so strong that he was not believed and he was therefore subjected to intense and prolonged interrogations. This lasted several days and then, eventually, he said the immortal words *Ich habe die papiere* (I have the papers). These were subsequently dug up in the back garden of his parents' home, secured in a bottle. The Allied powers now possessed the original and copies of Hitler's personal and political Wills plus the only copy of Goebbels' addendum. I was young at the time and so much of an extraordinary nature had happened in our Intelligence Section in such a short space of time that it was easy to ignore the whole significance. But little did I know that I was about to become involved in the case of yet another close contact of Adolf Hitler: the interrogation of Herman Karnau – a police officer in the bunker – and other Allied investigations into the death of Hitler.

On a freezing cold day in the winter of 1945, Rollo Reid called me to his office. He showed me a brief he had received from Colonel

Trevor-Roper. It contained a request to go to a hospital in Rotenburg, about thirty miles from Fallingbostel. My brief was to interrogate a patient by the name of Hermann Karnau who was present in the Bunker at Hitler's death. I demurred and said that this honour should go to one of my colleagues. Rollo with his usual charm insisted that the 'honour' should go to me. But worse was to come. We had no car and the only transport available was a motorbike. With no other option left, I set off on my journey.

Despite a bitterly cold and icy day I had no difficulties in finding the town and the hospital. A charming nurse showed me to the patient. Hermann Karnau looked pale and weak, lying in bed in a large dimly lit room. I introduced myself and he propped himself up, saying: 'I assume you have come to ask me about Hitler's death.' He explained that he had been one of the police guards ordered out of the Führer's bunker, but that he had changed his mind and returned. Finding the door locked, he had gone through the garden and entered the bunker by the emergency door where he met a colleague by the name of Erich Mansfeld who was on duty at the time. At that moment he turned and, to his surprise and shock, saw two bodies on the ground. Suddenly they burst into flames. Karnau concluded that they had been doused in petrol and someone had thrown a lighted match. He had a close look at the burning corpses and recognised them as being those of Adolf Hitler and Eva Braun. Hitler's head was smashed but recognisable. Karnau said that he returned several times, together with Mansfield, to watch the burning bodies. Karnau maintained that before shooting himself, Hitler had taken poison. Hilco Poppen, a guard in RSD-Dienststelle 1, also agreed that Hitler would never leave anything to chance. All this information was related to me by Karnau completely unemotionally.

On my homeward journey it grew colder. I drove through a blizzard and the extreme wind blew my hat away. Fortunately, the snow stopped but the intense wind and freezing conditions remained. As I had neither head nor ear protection I developed severe frostbite. On my return to Fallingbostel I immediately sought medical attention. The doctor had one look at my ears and expressed great concern, saying 'Young man, you are very lucky indeed. You could have lost your ears.' For the moment I had a terrible fright, but thanked the Almighty for being on my side.

We then received a brief from Trevor-Roper requesting us to interrogate two men. The first was Hilco Poppen and the second Erich Mansfeld. Both were former policemen who were in Hitler's bunker at the time of his suicide. In general, I found that the people who had been present in the bunker spoke in unity, agreeing that Hitler had taken poison before shooting himself. However, others who saw Hitler and Eva Braun after their deaths speculated at other possibilities. But that was all it was: speculation.

7

Intelligence and
Interrogation Work

In the spring of 1946 Captain Rollo Reid asked me to go to Munsterlager to take over the 43rd Intelligence Section, one of the largest discharge centres for German forces. The officer in charge of this section was going on well-deserved leave. Reid added that this officer was very conscientious and was reluctant to leave the section even for a short period, but had been pressurised to do so. I went by car and searched for the building which was to house my office and also my living quarters. A u-shaped driveway surrounded the impressively large house and I parked my car at the side. On entering the vast entrance hall a corporal introduced himself and showed me into two sizeable rooms situated on the ground floor to the right of the entrance. Both were for my personal use. I used the rear room as my bedroom, the other as a sitting room. The other ground-floor rooms were used as offices. Unpacking my small amount of luggage I made myself comfortable in my new 'palace'. A little later I had a chance to talk to the corporal that I had met earlier. He explained his function: 'I am the general factotum. However, amongst the many things I do, I am also responsible for the domestic personnel – the cook, the servants and the cleaners. I am also in charge of the daily and weekly rations and available for anything else you may wish me to undertake.'

I thought my offices were the most important rooms, however, he thought otherwise. 'Where are the office staff housed?' I asked him.

'Not in this building,' he said. 'If you want, I'll take you to the premises.'

A short distance away I noticed a lot of activity, people busily going in and out of a building, and discovered that this was the main office. A German civilian introduced himself to me in English as the office manager. He waved his hand to a tall, well-dressed man and explained that he was a medical practitioner in charge of all medical personnel in Munsterlager. He presented me to the rest of the staff, including the person who would act as my secretary, and then particularly drew my attention to a young man who was three or four years older than me and wearing thick glasses, saying that he was my interpreter. For the moment I thought it strange that an interpreter should be employed. I assumed that the officer I had temporarily replaced spoke insufficient German and had to employ a professional. A little later this man came over to me and began speaking in fluent English with a slight accent. He introduced himself as Perry Broad.

The name meant nothing to me. Why should it? And momentarily I was taken by surprise at his English-sounding name. I therefore asked him where he was born. He replied, 'In Brazil', and seeing that I still looked puzzled he continued by giving me short autobiographical notes. His mother, German by birth, married a Brazilian who had English ancestors. During the early part of the war his mother decided to return with him to Berlin and he became a student at the Humboldt University. Being called up by the German army, having bad eyesight and being regarded as politically unreliable because of his English connections, he was transferred to serve in the administrative section of the Auschwitz concentration camp. Immediately I heard this I was startled. I could not understand how British Intelligence in a sensitive area had employed this man. Seeing my reaction Perry Broad explained further. At first he had been arrested by the British, but after intensive interrogation he had been released and cleared of war crimes. He was then permitted to act as an interpreter for the British forces. He produced a fifty-six-page document (or diary) describing the most brutal activities carried out by the Kommandant and his guards at Auschwitz. After reading it I asked him to make six copies. I conducted further enquiries and they all resulted in assurances that Broad was most cooperative and definitely cleared of possible war crimes. I shall revert to the story of Perry Broad a little later.

The following procedure had been adopted at the Section before German army, navy and air force personnel were discharged from the internment camp: each person had a dossier giving details of their rank, service and location of where they had served. We had details of any German units suspected of war crimes and they were segregated and held in different compounds. The others followed a routine discharge procedure but were briefly interrogated before being released. I had about twelve interrogators working for me, all fluent German speakers. After a short interview, we exercised discretion and authorised the issue of discharge papers. If the interrogators had any doubts, the papers and the person was brought to me for further questioning and I then decided whether they qualified for release or should be detained for a period of either further interrogation or separated and taken to a camp dealing with potential war criminals. I attended the discharge area daily and, when any potential problem cases arose, I briefly examined the person further and took a decision whether to free him.

One day, a Dutch interrogating officer brought to me a short, blonde youth and explained that the boy professed to be a British national who had never served in the German forces. He claimed to have been wrongfully arrested and wanted to be discharged immediately. As the man did not speak German I questioned him in English and asked him to explain why he was in a German POW camp. He said the German police had accused him of stealing and, rather than being taken into German custody and tried in a German court, they had decided to put him into a German POW camp to be dealt with there. I asked him why he was in Germany and he answered that he was British and Jewish trying to trace a relative who he believed may have been in a concentration camp but had survived. While visiting a German town he was arrested and accused of theft. He assumed that the police, rather than bringing him to court and having a trial, thought the most expedient and less costly way of disposing of the matter would be to place him in the POW camp and let us sort out the matter. I asked him how he wanted me to deal with him. He suggested I put him on a train to Switzerland and let the British consulate pay for the return trip to the UK. I accepted his proposition and set him free.

To my amazement, I discovered this was a well-established method by the German police of dealing with awkward situations. Problems did arise of Germans trying to get their discharge with forged documents. I admired my team of interrogators who were able to spot those who either lied or produced forged documents, or who were inventive in constructing believable stories to obtain a quick release. The process could not be accelerated because of the very large number of detainees. The highly experienced team conscientiously took time to ensure no suspect was released before thorough investigation.

There were a number of attempted and successful suicides. If the latter, a post-mortem had to be conducted. I was invited to attend a post-mortem. On the one hand I did not wish to miss the opportunity, on the other, despite my front line service, I had not seen a dead body before. I summoned up some courage and agreed. The day arrived and I bravely presented myself at the makeshift mortuary. My new German friends, the office manager and the medical practitioner were already there. The body was wheeled in covered with a sheet. The pathologist whipped off the sheet and exposed the whitish-grey body. He told us the approximate time of death and that rigor mortis had set in. Briefly he explained how he would perform the post-mortem and, scalpel in hand, he proceeded to cut the chest open and fold the skin back. For a time I watched closely. He then proceeded to remove some organs, giving a lengthy explanation using German medical terms. I assume he thought we were all professional medical men. I managed to stay for about a quarter of an hour without any adverse affects. I then made my exit.

Evening came and dinner was served. For some inexplicable reason I had lost my appetite. I did not participate in the usual evening conversation but retired early. I went to bed but could not sleep. On my bedside table, so I imagined, lay a dead body. With the lights switched on I spent the rest of the night lying on the couch in the sitting room – so much for my bravery.

After a few days the corporal appeared and asked for permission to collect the usual rations of cigarettes, wine and spirits. I agreed and he disappeared, returning some time later with a massive supply. When I asked him why he had not distributed the full rations, he replied, 'I did.'

'Well, what are all these?' I asked.

He answered: 'They are yours.'

I counted about a dozen bottles of whisky, some gin followed by other spirits and many boxes of cigarettes and tobacco. I asked him to explain.

Although the team consisted of twelve people, the rations were indented for twenty-four. 'How come?' I asked.

Whenever somebody was posted elsewhere, his name remained on the list. If my arithmetic proved correct then twelve people must have left over a period of time, but yet still 'remained'. I understood. What I had failed to comprehend was why the officer in charge had not shared the loot with the rest of the staff. This would change from now on. Everyone would receive an extra ration with a recommendation that when I left the temporary post, the proper status quo would remain in force. That was my decision which I deemed fair and reasonable. The reason for the officer in charge's reluctance to take leave became perfectly clear. To go away meant paradise lost, never to be regained.

My learning process continued. The German office manager enjoyed other privileges. Release from the internment camp could be obtained or expedited by offering certain incentives to this manager; these could be defined in a number of ways. Here they are listed in his preference: 1) diamonds 2) jewellery 3) money (foreign of course). If the prisoner had a good-looking wife and she was willing she became priority No. 1. I had a suspicion that the doctor, in several ways, played an important part in these 'transactions'. For lists I signed of forthcoming releases I had to rely on medical reports supplied by the German MO. I recommended, what I am sure was a most unwelcome change, having two doctors sign the medical release recommendation papers. There were several reasons for this: first, it was to show them that I was not an easy touch; secondly, it put them on their guard; thirdly, above all, it was because I hate injustice in any form.

Returning to Perry Broad, his personality intrigued me. Of all the characters I had met in the past I was unable to classify him. Admittedly his background was unusual. He was completely different from the concentration camp personnel I had met before. Softly spoken, highly intelligent and cultured, he was articulate but had an unusual code of behaviour when foreign army personnel were present. He excused himself and moved out of the office whenever I had brief encounters with foreign officers and staff. I found this very strange. The only way I could understand his actions was by attributing it to a fear of Eastern Europeans. We encountered uneasiness when we liaised with the Russians, and this disquiet carried on to the staff, but not in such an extreme way as with him. A Yugoslav officer was a frequent visitor to our office and regarded as part of the establishment. Whenever he called, Perry Broad disappeared. At a later date this strange behaviour fell into place.

An added attraction was Perry Broad's artistry on the piano. I invited him to dinner and he discovered the keyboard. We both had a catholic taste in music. I asked him to play and he did, very well. It occurred to me to invite MacGarrety, the soprano saxophone player and my good friend in our section. With me playing violin and Perry Broad on piano, MacGarrety travelled fifty miles to be with us and played the sax. Jam sessions cemented our friendship and fostered a bond between us. I considered my stay in Munsterlager to be a learning and maturing process. Having power and responsibility at such an early age did not really sink in at the time. All this took place in the spring of 1946 and I was just twenty-one years old.

After about three to four weeks I returned to Fallingbostel from Munsterlager and continued my interrogation of internees. On the list of those I was to interrogate was ex-Gestapo officer Schroeder, who had once been assigned to Gestapo Security Manoeuvres. I was instrumental in getting Schroeder to write down his memoirs. Schroeder was a middle-aged man with greying hair and a friendly face. During the course of questioning he asked for permission to write down a short autobiography of his work which he considered would be very helpful. As he had a fascinating story to tell, which I thought would be of interest, I provided him with a small room in which to write.

He had joined the German police force in the middle of the 1920s as an ordinary policeman. In due course he was promoted to the equivalent of superintendent. In the early 1930s he became responsible for the prosecution of homosexuals in Berlin. He mentioned that there were 25,000 registered homosexuals in the Haupstadt, i.e. Berlin. At the time the figure seemed to be considerable and, therefore, it registered in my mind. Although during the Weimar Republic, he explained, there were fewer prosecutions, when the Nazis came into power homosexuality became a major offence and there were many arrests leading to imprisonment. In the latter part of the 1930s the German Army held manoeuvres and Schroeder was appointed police officer in charge of Security. Apparently, at that time, he and the general in charge of manoeuvres, General von Witzleben, struck up a conversation and seemed to establish a rapport. A short while later von Witzleben contacted him and they had a meal together. A lasting friendship was forged between them and he enlisted Schroeder's help in the following:

It transpired that a group of army officers needed to obtain information from the Gestapo. There were suspicions that the Gestapo had agents who had infiltrated the higher echelon of the army and von Witzleben asked Schroeder if he could investigate. After a short while it became obvious that the Gestapo indeed had infiltrated the army and had established a network of spies operating successfully within the German forces. Not surprisingly, therefore, this may have been the way Field Marshal Rommel's treachery was discovered. However, Schroeder at that time was more surprised when he realised a similar network of spies set up by the German army was operating within the Gestapo. In other words, everyone was happily spying on each other. Information had, and was, liberally going around in circles. Consequently, a policy decision had to be taken that anything of major importance, like a plot against Hitler, had to be confined to a much smaller and tighter circle.

After Schroeder finished writing his report we had a session of questions and answers. From experience I knew Hitler never failed to take action against anyone who plotted to remove him. My question to Schroeder was, therefore, 'Being aware of the danger emanating from the army hierarchy, it seems inconsistent for Hitler not to respond in his usual way.'

Schroeder answered that, in his opinion, arresting the army elite at that time would have severely interfered with and damaged his immediate aggressive plans in the east and possibly the west of Europe. The psychological, political and, above all, military consequences would have been immense. As long as he was still in control he could let matters simmer – but not explode. This appeared to be his prime aim at the time. Schroeder continued by explaining that the generals were bored with having little to do and were bound to cause unrest. Hitler had said: 'You must keep them well occupied and give them the exaltation as generals which they crave. That is their bread and butter.' During the war, von Witzleben had run the victorious campaign against France and Britain and was subsequently made a Field Marshal, with honours heaped upon him by Adolf Hitler. When military actions either simmered or turned sour, plans to get rid of Hitler were reactivated. From Schroeder's statement I concluded that the plot against Hitler may have been planned and a network already set up in the late 1930s. It is well known now that General von Witzleben was one of the major conspirators in the unsuccessful plot to kill Hitler. He was subsequently tried by a kangaroo court, found 'guilty' and shot.

Another internee connected to a high-ranking Nazi was brought into our camp at Fallingbostel. It was Hermann Goering's valet. I was assigned to interrogate him. I found it entertaining when, during the interview, he confided some of his boss's idiosyncrasies. He explained that Goering often went to bed between 2 or 3 a.m., and before retiring he would enjoy a substantial meal and, in particular, *bratwurst* (German sausage) and *kartoffelsalat* (potato salad). The Field Marshal's dress code also appeared very odd. He alternated between *lederhosen* (leather shorts) with *trachten* (national or peasant braces) and full Luftwaffen Field Marshal regalia, which he apparently designed himself. Goering would also go hunting on his vast estates wearing his own unique hunting outfit. As a memento the valet gave me Goering's nail clippers, which I treasured in a peculiar sort of way over the years, but sadly mislaid.

We had an excellent relationship with the officer in charge of the administration of the camp. He gave us every facility necessary to carry out our job efficiently and fully understood some of the difficulties we experienced. A number of the internees held were die-hard Nazis and obstructive. To have an officer in charge who was cooperative made our job considerably easier. Unfortunately, he was replaced and his successor, a major and a clergyman from Wales, failed to understand the many complexities experienced by us, especially from the unrepentant Nazis. After all, we were just a few miles away from Bergen-Belsen, where people were still suffering and dying from the atrocities perpetrated.

On one occasion, due to extremely bad weather, provisions reaching the camp were very much delayed. Consequently, rations to all internees were cut. The shortage of food was not confined to our internment camp but to the whole area. This led to a delegation from the inmates protesting about the scarcity. Particularly vociferous were those held in E Compound, in which there was a large percentage of die-hard Nazis. I was asked to go to this compound to deal with these prisoners. Arriving there, I found an organised revolt. A chorus of 'Hunger, hunger, hunger!' in German confronted me. I lost my calm, especially as I felt that those in E Compound were responsible directly or indirectly for the shortage of food. For a long time in occupied territories, which I had particularly seen in France and Holland during the Allied advance, many children had been starving and begging for food due to the scorched-earth policy of the Germans. Now I addressed these Germans who were revolting in E Compound, pointing out in no uncertain terms *their* responsibility for the shortage. I used strong language to describe them, namely *Abschaum der Menschheit* (scum of the earth).

It was too much for these 'delicate' souls to be addressed like this and they made a complaint to our righteous major who, without making any further enquiries, wrote to the colonel requesting my posting. As a result of this incident, we invited the major to dinner at our mess and enlightened him that the camp held prima facie war criminals and the elite Nazis were housed in E Compound. Although my friends tried to appease the major on my behalf, it had little effect. Colonel Proudlock sent a captain to make further investigations. I met him and explained the circumstances. He laughed and agreed that it was a 'storm in a teacup', and under no circumstances should I leave until I wished to.

Our section had an influx of civilians who were with the British Control Commission and the unit expanded. In overall charge was an intelligence officer class 2 (equivalent to a lieutenant colonel). The intimacy which had existed before now took a different form. For example, we instituted regular meetings and elected a chairman, secretary and minutes secretary. I was flattered when it was suggested that I act as chairman and was duly appointed. I had never held such an esteemed position before and had no idea what was involved. I had a shrewd inkling that I had to keep the peace between warring sections. However, to my amazement everything went swimmingly and the power which I envisaged did not materialise.

The hitherto informality and closeness did not completely disappear, but took a different form. To a certain extent it was understandable. A small group can function with an informal structure, but a much larger group would present difficulties. I became aware of an HM forces magazine published in the British Zone. To my astonishment I found an article by one of our new incumbents commenting on interrogation procedures which proved effective. It was very much based on a paper which I had given to him previously, setting out my methods – he had taken the credit for it. I started to think that it was now time to consider a move.

I applied to HQ for a posting. It did not take long to arrive and I made my way by train to Essen, the industrial part of the Ruhr. A pleasant young man in civvies with a slight Dutch accent met me at the station. He introduced himself as Jan. He was accompanied by a very friendly and beautiful red setter. The three of us jumped into a jeep, the dog comfortably in the back and me in the front seated next to Jan. The drive through Essen was, in a way, what I had expected. The central part of the town had been almost totally destroyed. Masses of rubble had not yet been removed and the pall of desolation still hung in the air. Understandably the Allies had concentrated their bombing on this highly industrialised area and there is, no doubt, that they did their job to perfection. Unfortunately, as in almost all industrial cities, the housing of the labour force surrounded the factories and so this section of the community took the brunt of the bombing.

It did not take long before the scenery changed very radically. We reached the Elysium fields – the hunting grounds of the industrial firms Krupps and Thyssen, where these 'kings' of industry had their palaces. Nothing was destroyed; everything was still standing. Beautifully manicured lawns surrounded lovely houses, those of the directors and senior management. The British intelligence section occupied a very nice residence in this area, a pleasant house surrounded by a well-kept garden. I was shown a comfortable room with a large balcony. Once again I unpacked my few belongings and made my way downstairs to meet some of my colleagues. They were very friendly and immediately invited me to come and have an afternoon swim. Swimming was not my normal scene but, not wanting to cause any initial disharmony, I obliged. We took a very short drive to a lake, a beautiful area with just a few properties surrounding it. The clear, warm water beckoned and we stripped off and swam. There were young, pretty girls and men laughing and having fun – I thought I had landed in Shangri-La.

The utopian world did not last very long. The next day we had a short briefing and I was introduced to the rest of the group. All my colleagues were ex-servicemen who had rejoined Control Commission. I was the only one still serving and, once again, the youngest. In overall charge was a Canadian by the name of Peters. From my experience, all the Canadians I had met during my army life were friendly, hospitable, easy to talk to and helpful. Peters was no exception. He appreciated that my mother language was, after all, German. All my colleagues understood and relied on that fact.

To my surprise I found Jan, my driver, was actually a colleague who spoke fluent German. He was cultured and, I discovered, came from a professional family. Whenever he introduced me to new surroundings we were accompanied by his dog. Wherever he went, the dog followed.

My fellow intelligence officers were an interesting and mixed bunch. They included a bearded gentleman, formally a naval officer with a tremendous sense of humour and full of risqué naval anecdotes; he had a fine voice and often regaled us with sea shanties. I never felt bored in his company. The senior member of our group was a former army major, our father figure, who never tired of giving me valuable and kindly advice; he was an excellent pianist which added to our entertainment. From time to time I accompanied him on the violin. It seemed to me that despite our varying ages and backgrounds the group gelled exceptionally well. However, I sometimes had the impression, rightly or wrongly, that there were hangovers from their service days; a questioning of authority and a jostling for position. I cannot recall being affected by this myself as I was still army personnel. Compared to my previous postings, I found the atmosphere in Essen less stressful and more relaxing. I no longer wore army uniform and I had use of a car. We lived comfortably in very lovely surroundings. Living in close proximity to these men with a fuller life experience became a maturing process, equipping me well for the future.

Peters asked me one day whether I would mind sharing my room temporarily with Sergeant Robert Reed. Part of the first floor where he occupied two rooms was being decorated. Intrigued as to why he had two rooms, while the rest of us had to make do with one, I asked him point blank why he was so privileged. Very simply he said that because he was an engineer, he required the extra room for his gear. He was a tall, bespectacled man of very pleasant disposition whose uniform appeared to be two sizes too big, but I accepted the explanation for the time being. After dinner, as was customary, we sat in the lounge, and after the usual small talk and discussion of the day's events we retired to our rooms. Still curious of Sgt Reed's function in our unit, I politely pumped him for further information. Before I could use my interrogational skills, my radio started to play up and developed a crackling noise. Without hesitation he offered to repair it, and I gladly accepted. The next day he entered into a sequence of mending and repairing each and every item that needed attention. This confirmed that he really was a qualified electrical engineer. I also observed that he was a very neat and tidy person: his clothes were immaculately folded, his shoes highly polished and his toiletries stored in an orderly fashion. Still not satisfied what his true function within our unit was, I continued with some subtle enquiries.

A few days later, when he appeared to be tired, I enquired whether he had had a hard time. The answer which I received seemed to fill another part of the jigsaw. He said he had been quite extensively using binoculars, which proved very strenuous. I temporarily stopped questioning him. Then he talked freely about his family life. He was happily married with two teenage children and enjoyed a successful career in electronics. His priority seemed to be his family, as at every available opportunity he would telephone or write home. He seemed to lead a more or less conventional life.

During the early part of the war, Sgt Reed had served with the Royal Engineers and was stationed in the Midlands and in London. After the Allied invasion of France in June 1944, he had remained in London until the war was almost finished and had received his posting to intelligence only a short while later. His knowledge of German was mediocre but then I thought it was mainly his engineering skills rather than his linguistic skills that were in demand. Although it was originally planned that Reed would remain with us for just a week or so, Peters apologised to me saying that the job required at least a fortnight longer. Again this caused further confusion as to Reed's real assignment. Gradually, I began to enjoy Sgt Reed's company in the evenings. We talked a great deal about the theatre, music and current affairs. This constituted a very pleasant change to the style of conversation with my colleagues. But he was still an enigma despite our continuous daily contact. The true object of his stay with us remained a puzzle until things finally started to fall into place. Immediately after our evening meal he would retire to our joint living quarters and write at length. Originally I thought these were letters home, but being an excessive amount of writing I realised this could not be so. Instead they were reports of his daily activities.

After Robert Reed had left the camp, Peters and I discussed at some length his stay with us. His odd, perhaps even bizarre behaviour, such as to lock himself in a room all day long, coupled with his continuous silence of what he did and the bag of tools and equipment he carried with him, can only be understood as symptoms of the time we lived in. Eventually, we discovered the situation. The house that Reed had under surveillance turned out to be a clandestine and well-camouflaged black market centre, with coffee being the main commodity imported. Now accepted as a complete triviality, this was then regarded as sinister and undercover. However, it highlighted a number of characteristics so prevalent in Germany during the very early years of the Second World War. It was well concealed, kept top secret and called the Fear of Authority – a distinct Nazi legacy, some may even more appropriately call it a German illness, lying dormant from earlier days and being psychopathic.

Furthermore, in line with the current trend of varied illegal activities distinctly defined as *lebenswichtig* (in order to live), minor misdemeanours were reported instantly and continuously. Jealousy among civilians, exceedingly common at the time, led to a system of informing on neighbours to the occupying forces, almost daily, oddities classified as offences. Misdemeanours, seen as anti-social behaviour anywhere else, became known here as a severe violation and a clear offence. Similarly, mild felonies regarded as meek eccentricities were now deemed to deserve strict punishment. Justice had wide or narrow definitions determined by the needs of the moment. All this could be excused as the rule to exist. So the law had been given acceptable definitions. The Allies equally had guidelines which they strictly or loosely abided by. You had to govern in a democratic way. You had to show true democracy in action as a contrast to the Nazi regime that had governed Germany for thirteen years. We wanted to introduce democracy but had to use dictatorial means to enforce it. This was an anachronism.

In the second part of 1946, the hunt for Nazi war criminals went on although not with the rigour and intensity of the previous year. There was a long list of heinous evildoers, such as Eichmann and Mengele, who were still at large and the search continued unabated. Work ethics and directions changed, now assigned to fight communism, the new enemy lurking in the east of Europe. Intelligence needed an organisational shift to counter these new conditions. And consequently, a new structure was designed. Thought was given to define who the new enemy was. So far all efforts had been made to emasculate the German threat. Questions were raised – 'Has that been achieved? Has the Nazi threat been erased and substituted by the new communist menace?' The organisational energy had to be channelled to a danger which had not been clearly defined. What was needed was the collective help of intelligence and counter-intelligence to probe and assess how strong these real or imaginary threats were. Radical structural changes took place. The Control Commission took over intelligence work which hitherto was the prerogative of the Army Intelligence

Corps – understandably so since there was more and more contact with the German Government and studies to be made

At this time a new problem arose, namely illegal migration to Palestine. Inevitably, searches were made and my CV revealed my close connection with Palestine. My immediate family was now living in Rehovot not far from Tel Aviv. Above all, I had made an application soon after my conscription in 1944 to join the Jewish Brigade. A request was made that I should temporarily report to a unit stationed near Hamburg which was in need of some urgent assistance. On arrival I entered the inner sanctum: a medium-sized, brightly lit room. It looked like a very busy telephone exchange, but in reality turned out to be a well-organised listening post. Men with headsets were seated on one side of the room, listening in to conversations and decoding messages. The officer in charge approached me and asked whether I was Rothman, the Hebrew speaker. My reply was in the affirmative. I was first asked to translate some messages which appeared to be innocuous, such as, 'baby girl arrived safely – *mazel-tov*' or 'sorry can't be with you but Happy Birthday'; also, 'boy seven and a half pounds arrived Tuesday', which to me could be construed as a coded communication. I felt very uncomfortable considering my own mother and brother had entered Palestine 'illegally', and after receiving several similar telegrams for translation I made my feelings known to the CO and asked to be relieved of this duty. He understood fully and I returned to Essen.

Reverting to the girls from Bergen-Belsen, who we had entertained in our mess in the summer of 1945, I knew that they had gone illegally to Palestine because they had written to me. It has to be understood this was the height of illegal immigration. Europe, especially Central Europe, was a huge transit camp. Those liberated from concentration camps had an acute problem. To return to their homes anywhere in Eastern Europe was impossible. In many cases their neighbours had been the informers and were instrumental in their incarceration in the death camps. A popular saying grew up amongst Jews: *Jude wohin?* (Jews where to?); and a very popular Yiddish song became *Woahin soll ich gehn?* (Where shall I go?). During the latter part of 1945, around 710,000 displaced persons were in the British Zone in Germany and Austria. To reduce this number substantially became an immense problem. Some wished to remain, others of whom were Jewish wished to emigrate to Palestine, and some of Polish origin wanted to rejoin or trace their families and resume their life in their former homeland. They soon realised that life under the communist regime was totally alien to what was expected and they returned to Germany.

In Berlin during the war, about 8,000 Jews had managed to escape arrest by hiding or being hidden. My school friend Hans Rosenthal, who later became a very famous German TV personality and presenter, told me an extraordinary story of survival. At the start of the war he was my age, fourteen years old. On his way home from school one day he saw the police at the door of his apartment. As he approached he was signalled to disappear quickly. He returned home later in the day to find the police waiting for him. He was arrested and taken to the local train station for transport. While standing on the platform, the two policemen told him to wait for them while they had some refreshments. Understandably, he did not hang around, but ran off and disappeared. He felt the police had deliberately given him the opportunity to escape. He spent the rest of the war hiding in garden sheds on allotments in Berlin where he was helped to survive by a number of German women who provided him with food and other necessities.

Hans's father had died before the war and his mother tragically died of cancer in 1941. His brother Gert and the rest of his family died in the camps. In 1945, immediately after the war had finished, Hans Rosenthal found a job working for the RIAS (the radio station controlled by the American occupying forces) as an odd-job boy, which included sweeping floors and making coffee. He was a very intelligent lad and quickly worked his way up. Ultimately, he became one of Germany's best loved and favourite TV personalities, like Terry Wogan and the late Eamon Andrews. He wrote, acted, presented and directed many popular TV programmes; in particular *Dalli Dalli* which ran from 1971 to 1986. He was responsible for the catchphrase so popular in Germany: *Sie sind der meinung, das war …?* (So you all think that was …?). The TV audience would loudly respond: *Spitze!* (Tops).

He was an active member of the Council of Jews in Germany as well as being involved with many other charitable organisations. He was awarded several honours, which included the Federal Cross of Merit, Goldene Kamera and Telestar. The square in front of the RIAS building was named Hans Rosenthal Platz, and a sports centre in Berlin-Charlottenburg has also been named after him. Additionally, a blue plaque has been fixed to the building where Hans spent his childhood.

Hans married a very good-looking, charming and likeable German lady by the name of Traudl. They had two children: a son (a lawyer in Berlin) and a daughter. Hans sadly died an early death from cancer at the age of sixty-two. All the leading German dignitaries attended his funeral, including the then German Chancellor. He is buried in the same Berlin cemetery as my parents. As I visit the cemetery quite frequently, I also visit his grave which is nearby. Some years ago my wife and I were invited to attend the 225th anniversary of my school in Berlin (Judische Mittleschuler Grosse Hamberger Strasse) and part of the festivities included a visit to the opera. Nearby sat Traudl who, during the interval, and to our pleasant surprise, introduced us to Prinz Hohen-Zollen, a descendant of the Kaiser.

A sadder story of survival was that of my best friend Siegfried (Siggy) Mandelkern. In October 1939 my father and Siggy were both arrested and incarcerated in Sachsenhausen concentration camp at Oranienburg, not far from Berlin. Before their arrest they were advised to sew money into the lining of their clothing and this was done by Siggy's father who was a men's tailor. In April/May 1940, through the intervention of Herr Belgart and with the help of the money sewn into their clothing, both my father and Siggy were released. They were strongly advised by Belgart to leave Berlin and Germany immediately. My father did so. But Siggy did not. This was understandable as he was the only child of elderly parents and his father was disabled. He stopped with his parents and they delayed him leaving. He ended up taking a different route to my father and made his way south-east to Poland. At some point he was challenged by the Polish police. He panicked and started to run away, so they shot him. His parents survived by being hidden in attics by compassionate Germans who risked their own lives to help them. Immediately after the war finished, the parents returned to their flat and waited hopefully for Siggy to return.

During one of my visits to Berlin, a search revealed that Mr and Mrs Mandelkern had survived. I went to their home and knocked on the door. They opened it and shouted, 'Siggy!' Tragically – and disappointingly for them – it was me. Despite their frustrated expectation they embraced me and cried bitterly. Still with tears in their eyes they confessed that every time they opened the door they visualised Siggy standing there. I did not reveal my suspicions, for even I remotely hoped he had survived. I visited Mr and Mrs Mandelkern again. This time they invited me to accompany them to a displaced persons camp where they organised the distribution of food and clothing. This admirable elderly and frail couple put aside their own sorrows and helped others in greater need. Now reflecting on the past, and in particular on the period shortly after the war's end, when the everyday scene appeared to change swiftly and dramatically, time and events followed one another so quickly they could not be fully digested. People you knew before the war were not the same afterwards. Hans achieved fulfilment, but the Mandelkerns despair. Many things compensated Hans for the loss of his family, but what compensated the Mandelkerns? The contrasts are too immense. If one views the happenings in retrospect they take on different proportions.

Of great concern was how to differentiate between the genuine asylum seekers and those masquerading as asylum seekers. Many Nazis escaped by pretending to be Holocaust survivors. The number of Germans applying for permission to leave Germany became overwhelming, and the weaning out of Nazis and collaborators was soon an insurmountable task. When doubts arose, they were arrested and sent to intelligence for further investigation. The number of informers grew. Some were genuine and wished to help; others, having a grudge against a neighbour, built up what appeared to be a prima facie case and reported them. So numerous were the complaints that instead of assisting the Allies they became a hindrance. Our intelligence section and others were overloaded and, as a result, genuine Nazi criminals escaped the net, innocents were detained, with a surfeit of headaches for us in particular and for the British administrators in general. Unable to ignore the reports, every avenue had to be explored. For example, we received information of clandestine meetings of ex-Nazis who had set up an escape route to South America. It sounded plausible but it warranted further investigation. The news came via informants who had previously supplied us with valuable information. Together with a colleague I drove to a lower-middle-class area in the suburbs of Essen. We parked the car and walked about a hundred yards to an empty house.

My colleague entered the house and climbed the stairs to the first floor and from there watched while I crossed the road to the address which had been given to us. I was quite nervous as I knocked. To add to this, a grim-looking man in shirtsleeves opened the door and asked me in a local dialect: '*Was wollen sie?*' (What to you want?). The following conversation then ensued. Responding in German with a Berliner accent, I asked whether I could come in and speak to him in confidence. He nodded and showed me into a dark sparsely furnished room. He told me to sit down and asked the purpose of my visit. I explained that I was interested in leaving the country, possibly going to South America. He listened in silence. I asked if he could help me. He wanted to know who had given me his address and I replied that as it was given to me in confidence, I could not reveal my source. A door opened and another man entered. They whispered together and I heard the words 'He is from Berlin.' The second man then left the room but I was almost certain that he had been listening in on us. After a short conversation I felt my questioner became somewhat suspicious. I wrote down in *suetterlin* (a style of copperplate writing introduced in Prussia in 1915 and assiduously promoted by the Hitler regime throughout Germany) a forwarding address. I placed it on the table and left. My colleague and I returned to the office and I wrote a report expressing my opinion and recommending a follow-up. As a result a watch was put on the house. To this date I still ponder: were they Nazis or were they not?

From time to time we had to deal with a miscellany of routine enquiries received from other intelligence sections or units inside the British, French or American zones. For example, we received from the CIA requests from German nationals who wished to marry American soldiers. Careful and often painstaking enquiries had to be made as to the suitability of the applicants. This may have been considered one of the easy escape routes used by Nazis or people alleged to have committed war crimes. We had to call in the applicants on every occasion and submit them to a mild form of interrogation. If it warranted further investigation we informed the enquirer, instituted a further search and communicated the results and our assessment. On several occasions, the good-looking, articulate and apparently nice girl turned out to be someone with a rather murky past.

Of great help to my interrogation technique was the time spent during my adolescence in Gwrych Castle in North Wales, where I encountered people from all parts of Germany with differing local German dialects. The boys and girls had had nicknames based on idiomatic expressions they used, or their place of origin, i.e. 'Dresden' or 'Leipzig', and one boy from the southern part of Germany was called *ische hause* which meant 'at home' – it appeared to be a common local expression. This became one of my important interrogation tools. If someone alleged to have spent the war years in a particular place I was able to spot whether they had picked up the local dialect. If not, I knew they were trying to spin a yarn. Language and accent revealed a great deal, perhaps not as much as it would in Britain.

In our interrogation methods we exploited the innate fear prevalent in the Germans in our zone of being handed over to the Russians. For example, if difficulties were experienced with an uncooperative detainee, I simply lifted up the telephone and requested the secretary to bring in the forms of transfer to the Russian Zone. The secretary entered, handed me some forms and I would start to ask additional fitting and more detailed questions. Invariably it did the trick. There was a continuous influx of pitiful young and old, emaciated and disheveled German POWs, who had been released from the Russian Sector, telling appalling stories of their treatment. How truthful they were was difficult to assess. Were they soliciting sympathy? However, it should never be forgotten the extreme suffering, deprivation, misery and hardship inflicted by the Germans on the Russian people. Many, many millions died. I always bore in mind that I was neither judge nor jury and that my main object was to try to ascertain the truth. A number of people I had to interrogate often suffered from a non-collective or paranoiac collective guilt and this presented difficulties. They had elected a government who openly expressed its hatred for minority groups which contributed vastly in many fields of life – socially, politically, culturally and economically. As long as these criminal leaders were successful they had the full backing of a large majority of the people; barring a small minority, the population was contented and supported the regime. It was an endless learning and maturing process. It helped to form my *Weltanschauung* (philosophy of life).

Sometime in 1946 I was given to understand that I could apply for British citizenship. I completed the necessary forms and several months later was invited to appear in front of a panel consisting of a brigadier as the chairman, a colonel and a major. This became a memorable occasion. I entered a well-lit room with a long table. The three men in their impressive uniforms studied a number of papers and then asked for a short confirmation of my pre-army and present army days. This was followed by questions concerning my parents. They said: 'They live in Palestine, we understand?'

'Yes,' I replied and gave a brief description of when and how they arrived there. I did not expect anything further on the subject but to my surprise they continued their line of questioning.

'Is your father a member of the Irgun Zvi Leumi [a Jewish terrorist organisation]?'

I replied, 'Of course not.'

They persisted: 'Why do you say – of course not?'

I amplified this by saying that my father had suffered eight months in a concentration camp, a further year in confinement in a football stadium on the island of Rhodes and subsequently had been interned by the Italians. My father was only too anxious to lead a peaceful existence for the rest of his life. This was followed by similar questions about my mother. My answer was that she had also suffered from Nazi domination and was one of the passengers on a boat that had been blown up in Haifa harbour. I recalled the story of the *Patria* which had resulted in the loss of 250 lives. At the time, I thought that these three high-ranking officers were asking me – an intelligence officer – completely unintelligent questions. Had my parents been members of a terrorist organisation would it be likely for my reply to be 'yes'?

There was a momentary silence from all three of them and then a somewhat mundane question followed: 'What do you wish to do when you leave the army?' I responded by saying that I wished to pursue a career in journalism. Before I left they smiled at me, gave me a reassuring nod and bid me farewell. I saluted and left. Two or three months later, in early 1947, I became a British citizen while still in the army.

It was during 1947 that I was posted to two towns in the northern part of the Ruhr, Muenchen-Glattbach and Krefeld. By now I was intelligence officer class 3 (equivalent to the rank of captain) working for British Control Commission assigned to industrial intelligence. My brief was to investigate industrial espionage and sabotage, and in that role I had to attend conferences and meet my counterparts from the other Allied zones. We exchanged information of interest to each other. The main office was situated in a large private house which had belonged to an aristocratic German family, but was subsequently requisitioned and occupied by a high-ranking Nazi. After his arrest, British Intelligence had moved in and some of the rooms in this magnificent edifice became offices. The enormous bathroom with a gigantic sunken bath on the ground-floor level became a feature. On rare occasions, and purely out of curiosity to spot how much water was needed to fill this monstrous tub, we started filling it. Not, however, to capacity as this would have led to the outside water reservoir being drained, or the River Rhine losing so much water as to leave boats stranded. Purely to stem the consequences it remained on display as a landmark of past wealth. To quote a German poem so apt which came to my mind: *Noch diese eine Seule zeugt von verschwunderer Pracht auch diese schon geborsten kann stuertzen uber Nacht*, which means 'This single column bears witness to past splendour but even this one so rickety can collapse overnight'. I occupied an office in the Gneisenaustr. 44 Muenchen-Glattbach, and another office in Krefeld in the Milgov building.

To this day I am not aware of anyone being transferred to the British Control Commission, a quasi-civilian organisation, while still remaining in His Majesty's Forces. It appeared to be unique. While all my colleagues drew reasonable and acceptable salaries, I received a pittance in comparison. Admittedly, though, I enjoyed many other benefits, such as almost complete freedom of action and indescribable power relative to many of my other colleagues in the Army, with no one to salute or say 'sir' to. I realised it was temporary and it felt like being handed out small gifts for which I had to be eternally grateful.

I desperately needed civilian clothes. Before disbanding my uniform I searched for a competent German tailor. I found one, but the need to find material still remained. For anyone else it may have appeared an immense problem but not so for a British intelligence officer. Bribery and corruption, an integral part of German life then, still existed. To obtain favours you needed valid currency but more so – connections. By knowing me, you automatically had access to both. Obtaining good-quality clothes, still difficult for most, fortunately presented no problem for me. Appearance, including colour, not quality, mattered to me most and this was the criterion when buying my suits for all occasions. Consequently, I picked grey, blue and brown. For advice and guidance I enlisted the help of my friend Alec Bergenthal whose father was a top tailor and designer. He suggested wide shoulders, a long double-breasted jacket and trousers with turn-ups. This information I duly conveyed to my 'man' who produced the finished article. What did I look like? It depended on who you were and where you came from. To the German public they saw me, no doubt, as a well-groomed Englishman. To the conventional British they would call me, aptly a self-styled, pompous and conceited 'spiv'. To the real spiv I was one of them but fairly obviously a bloody foreign spiv. The realisation came very much later when my girlfriend, who later became my wife, honestly and not so politely told me what I really looked like. I then studied friends and colleagues and saw how they dressed, in respectable, inconspicuous and moderately coloured apparel. I quickly disposed of the three treasured garments. All of a sudden I could afford it.

Germans were greatly impressed by names and titles. As my clientele consisted mainly of such people it sounded hugely impressive when I signed my formal correspondence 'H. Rothman' and underneath 'Intelligence Officer', or at times put simply the word 'Mr' in front of my name, doing the same with my visiting cards. A Hochdeutsch accent, which I deliberately cultivated, caused an enigma, in particular amongst the people I interrogated or occasionally socialised with. Nothing could be more disturbing than that, and I render my belated apologies.

Jealousy is a trend I believe more found amongst Germans than other people I have encountered. This worked very much in my favour as an interrogation method. I forget who the informer was but I was told that a relatively young man who practised medicine in the Homburg area belonged to the Nazi Party. So I asked him to come to my office. He immediately obliged and admitted that he had initially had a surgery in Berlin and as such received the title of SA Sturmfuehrer (equivalent of Lieutenant). The membership and rank qualified him for arrest and certainly prevented him from practising, so he moved as far as possible from Berlin to Homburg, here in West Germany, and understandably concealed his rank. Young and successful, with a pretty wife and a young family, he was the envy of middle and senior age colleagues, who had given him away. As a conscientious doctor he kept abreast with the advance of his profession and attended lectures. The medical profession, with the discovery of Penicillin moved fast, especially in mid-1945 when the exchange of notes became possible.

When he came to see me he impressed me with his honesty by admitting his SA past and I understood the reason for his concealment. Checking the particulars he gave me and after meeting his young family I believed his story. The need for people engaged in medicine was also an important factor and I allowed him to continue practising. Not so taintless was that I retained him as an informer. After all, that was my job. What happened to him and his family? In 1958, while on holiday in this area, I tried to trace him and his family. They had moved but fortunately not very far. When I knocked at the door of the house it was opened by his wife, who told me that not long before, her husband, while on a skiing holiday in Austria, had suffered a major heart attack and died. Sadly, she was then left with the young family.

In Bad Homburg our offices were in a prime position in the town. They looked bright, neat and impressive. From the window of my office, on the first floor of this modern four-bedroom house, there was a beautiful view, which at times I found distracting. She had medium-blonde hair, was tall with a nice figure and spoke English quite well. She became my Secretary. When she introduced herself she mentioned that she was engaged and soon to be married – this was not uncommon and a standard phrase I had heard before. She worked well and finished all her work on time.

Our small intelligence unit provided a vital link in the Northern Ruhr to the revival of the textile industry, and we played an important part in seeing that this was carried out without 'snags'. I succeeded in getting the cooperation of newly established entrepreneurs. Workers and employers worked in apparent harmony. I attended board meetings and Union meetings as an observer. It was in everyone's interest to revive and foster the smooth running of the industry. The small town lacked cultural interests but the larger, more cosmopolitan towns were not too far away.

To relieve any possible boredom, parties were essential. Male attendance had to be augmented by female company. The small band, like many in Germany, very quickly acclimatised to the needs of the Allied Forces and the music of Glenn Miller, Harry James and the Dorsey Brothers soon entered the dance scene. I invited my new secretary to one such dance and she came, without her fiancé. When we needed a change of scenery, a river trip with dinner dancing became part of the itinerary. We had a good time.

We had two German security guards who guarded our offices and living quarters. One shift ran from early evening through the night and the other during the day. During one late afternoon, after returning exhausted from an interesting meeting with leading German textile manufacturers, I decided to postpone my report to HQ. After a quick meal I retired to the lounge and fell asleep. A loud knocking on the front door woke me, and the night watchman apologised saying he had mislaid his keys and asked whether I had a spare set that he could borrow. I retrieved a set for him and noticed he spoke with a cultured and refined Berlin accent, completely uncharacteristic for someone working as a security guard. Looking closely he had a gentle and intelligent face, which again was inconsistent with the job he was doing.

I started a conversation with him and discovered he was a former UFA film director and actor. Anyone who had lived in Central Europe and beyond knew about UFA. What, for heaven's sake, was he doing here carrying out such menial work? He was eager to talk and a fascinating story unfolded. He explained that the film industry had held a great attraction for young people – especially during the war years and shortly after. Entertainment back then had consisted of films, classical and light music concerts, ballets, plays, sport, variety shows, radio, the playing of 78 RPM records and, in particular, ballroom dancing. On paper it sounded a lot, but most of the items listed were produced and shown on a small scale, and in localities, such as bombed areas or makeshift premises, making it difficult for the public to reach. Pleasant surroundings created atmosphere giving this 'extra' to the entertainment. Now, Hollywood dominated the industry and was freely available to the German public; an abundance of mediocre movies were churned out, with the occasional gem.

The British motion picture industry, however, despite tremendous difficulties, turned out remarkable films. The price paid for a cinema ticket was affordable by almost everyone. Two film shows for the price of one, with a newsreel thrown in – it was certainly a bargain. Most topics of discussion started with 'Did you see Betty Grable in her latest film?', or 'Have you seen *Brief Encounter*?' Invariably, a heated debate followed a fiery evaluation of whether this or that was worth seeing. Those with money to burn saw two shows per week and those with limited resources, which included me, saw only one and were forced to be selective. This was a factor in the decline of the German film industry. During the war, UFA had fulfilled the role of Hollywood in the German-speaking territories. The import of films from abroad being censored and restricted by Hitler's regime meant they became a much sought-after commodity for those opposed to the Nazis. For those anxiously seeking excellence, it became a rarity. UFA displayed reasonable quality and had the byword for a good film. When I discovered this middle-aged man's connection with UFA he immediately shot up in my esteem, but with a question mark attached. What was he doing here? I needed to know a lot more.

He explained that the German picture industry gradually dissolved and, although there were signs of revival, many found themselves out of work and had to seek employment in other fields. Nothing suitable had been offered to him and, as he said quietly and sadly, 'I have to live'. He added that he was also a successful 400-metre runner and had represented Germany in a number of races. As I believed his story, and felt help was needed, I thought of employing him in a more constructive and remunerative way. His knowledge of acting would come in useful and before long we had a perfectly suitable job for him. I got him involved in the investigations involving Nazis escaping to South America. Instructions were given to arrest a German who was suspected of taking a leading part in this scheme. However, some further evidence was needed so that we could build up a case. Here our UFA friend became useful, and we asked him to use his acting experience. Under the pretext of being a welfare officer, supplying provisions to inmates at the prison where the suspect was held, he was told to befriend the target. Through him we solicited vital information, which led to Operation Tango.

Previously, in a briefing at headquarters, we had been told about an organisation currently active in our area that was helping former Nazis to leave the country. They were being smuggled out of Germany to destinations in South America. A route operated quite legitimately for bona fide emigrants wishing to leave the British Zone, but some ex-Nazis found it a convenient way of fleeing the country and thereby escaping prosecution. They were equipped with false papers which were hard to detect. Living for a brief period in a temporary camp, they were interrogated and if cleared, supplied with transport to Argentina or other countries in South America. Some were suspected of possessing funds stolen, most probably, from Jews, Gypsies and others under German occupation. One should not forget there was also a small section of decent Germans who opposed the Nazi regime and fought in underground movements. Their fate was similar to Jews, i.e. arrested and sent to concentration camps, in which the majority no doubt died.

Operation Tango, which had been planned for nightfall, duly arrived. An appeal for the army to help resulted in the arrival of a dozen soldiers in armed vehicles ready to surround the large camp. Five of us from the Control Commission turned up in private limousines dressed in civilian clothes. Tables and chairs were provided for us and it all looked very impressive. The army carried out a thorough search of the camp and we interrogated people with negative results. All appeared to have legitimate documents, including entrance visas mainly for Argentina, Uruguay and Chile. No one named on our list could be found; if they had been there then they had now vanished. To have at least arrested and then released a few would have saved face. On reflection it was badly planned and impulsive. Occasional raids on camps with armed personnel and a small group of intelligence officers proved of little success. That was the way Eichmann, Mengele and other high-ranking Nazis escaped the net. Thankfully, the failure could not be attributed to me.

The time of my demob approached. It was open to me to stay on, but I could see no future in Control Commission and I very much looked forward to civilian life. I continued my active service in the British forces until the autumn of 1947.

8

Civilian Life

In October 1947 I was demobbed and returned to England. Ahead of me lay a difficult time of adjustment and the search for employment. I had had my education disrupted under the Nazi regime and so the choices open to me appeared to be limited. Grants and monetary help were only offered to those who had studied their subject prior to entering the army, so the rule book said. I wished very passionately to study psychology but without financial assistance it remained a pipe-dream. Similarly, the study of music was vetoed. Going through the list of courses which I *could* afford, I came across an opening in Economics and business administration which included social psychology. This had some attraction so I decided to go for it. A similar course was available in Cambridge. But who did I know there? I feared losing my existing friends, so eventually I decided to opt for a London college. Many years later, on reflection, maybe it appeared the wrong choice. In my defence my decision was influenced by a schoolteacher nicknamed Heiko. He decried the Oxbridge universities by saying, 'it's all glitter but no gold', or something along those lines. I needed sound advice which was absent at the time.

I enlisted at London's Westminster College, St Margaret's branch. I waited to be called up for the start of term but, on receiving no summons, I telephoned the secretary and was told the semester had started some time ago. I had missed almost a whole term but seemed to get into the swing of it quickly. I found college life in England exceedingly different from school life in Berlin. My fellow students were a strange assortment with some willing to work hard, others lackadaisical in their approach and others who came purely for the ride and the money. There were those who pretended to live in lodgings, receiving the top pay but actually still lived at home. They arrived for lectures in modern sports cars; they dressed flamboyantly in line with their status, wearing fashionable sports jackets, flannels and the regulation college scarf slung around their necks; and at interim examination times they failed to turn up, producing a doctor's certificate claiming they were unwell. Several were married and had children and, therefore, qualified for the top grants.

I felt I had a problem. Being a relatively short time after the end of the war, the anti-German feelings were still very strong. Hence I avoided admitting my German birth. In addition, I concealed my parents' association with Palestine. Terrorist activities there had led to declining sympathy for Jews. I attributed this as a welcome excuse for the Gentile world at not coming to the rescue of Jews during the earlier part of the Nazi regime. The Irgun played into the hands of those who claimed justification for being silent when the Jewish communities cried out desperately for help. This mitigated guilt gave the silent majority the much-needed and looked-for excuse. How stupid must I have been for concealing my true origin? Reflecting on this in later years I can only claim my somewhat odd behaviour to several factors, which produced a temporary change so alien to me. An objective and honourable self-psychoanalysis would be difficult or a sheer impossibility.

During this time I read a Blue Penguin edition of a book, the title of which was something like *Scientific Attitudes*. It demolished every form of subjectivity and only allowed rational thought and objectivity. Art and music put under scrutiny became dull and, therefore, unacceptable to a 'rational mind'. It produced by-products, such as excuses for an undisciplined life, hitherto controlled, religious and ethical, and excuses for lapses in my regular, composed lifestyle. This foreign and fortunately brief period I did not shrug off immediately, but after slowly thinking it through and realising it may cause harm and have an ill effect, I adopted a philosophy more easily digestible and manageable. Was it late adolescence? On reflection, very likely so, and part of mental growth.

In the educational field I came to grips with, what was to me then, a somewhat alien subject, i.e. economics. I even began to like it. Our very left-wing lecturer added to this. Everything he taught seemed to make sense and fell into my understanding of the existing social-ist world. I also admired another lecturer by the name of Hughes. From time to time we had lunch together and my love for the subject earned me high marks. To my great surprise I won a prize of £10, a colossal amount in those days, for being top pupil for my essay on the 'Distribution of Raw Materials and Money Reaching Britain by Way of a Triangular Journey'. Not only did I respect the lecturer, he enjoyed discussions with me and I found the subject very stimulating and thought-provoking. The elderly teacher on business administra-tion and management taught in a conventional and acceptable way. One could judge the popularity of a lecturer by the regular attendance figures. A good audience meant an interesting subject, good delivery and an acceptable personality of the lecturer or speaker.

What I found strange, but so typically English, was the fact that teach-ing was interrupted in order to announce the latest test score. The love of cricket undoubtedly affected the attendance figures at lectures. Announcing scores regularly attracted a large audience. For the first time, I realised the importance of this sport to the British people. Nothing was too sacred that it could not be interrupted by the announcement of cricket scores; nothing was more holy than Bradman hitting either a century or being bowled out for a duck. Jubilation and disruptions were permissible at all times when the game was in progress. Otherwise, boring lectures gave a good opportunity to complete *The Times* or *Telegraph* crossword.

There were, unfortunately, infrequent visits to the London School of Economics. If opportunities existed to hear Harold Lasky then we were advised well in advance and recommended to go as early as possible. The lecture hall was always crowded to capacity and the man in question was surrounded by an air of immortality – so sanctified were the names of these selected few. All this has disappeared now and nobody will be enshrined in the secluded heaven of saintly Professors of Economics.

Harold Campbell, who had been such an influence on me before the war, reappeared in my life. Although I never completely lost contact with him while 'touring the continent in or out of uniform', I only encountered him at irregular intervals and for short periods. By now he had been appointed the assistant secretary of the Cooperative Party. The offices of the Cooperative Party were in London's Victoria, while my college was in Horseferry Road. He frequented the British restaurant situated at equal distance between us and it became our regular meeting place. He later succeeded Sir Jack Bailey as the secretary, and like him was offered a knighthood, but declined. He had a vast fund of stories to tell which I just lapped up.

I was often astounded at the pompous behaviour of some of the dignitaries he mixed with and knew well. It did, in many ways, disturb and transform my idealistic conception of true socialism. Simply, it did not exist. What's more, it exposed a reality which I, as a naive young man, found disappointing or at times shattering. On the other hand, my experience since leaving my family and Germany should have shown me very clearly that my utopian world which I thought would be coming immediately after the war was a fantasy. My frequent conversations with Harold confirmed that. The Holocaust left an unexpected mark on him. He confessed to me that had he known of the horrendous atrocities committed by Hitler in the Holocaust, along with my own personal experiences and the sadness connected with my parents, he would not have been a conscientious objector.

Laurie Pavitt, who shortly afterwards became Member of Parliament for Brent, was an occasional lunch companion with us. I knew him quite well from my pre-army days, as he was a long-standing friend of Harold Campbell and Joe Banks. Laurie and Harold later formed a group known as The Walk and Talk Club, which became the Shuffle and Grunt Club, but I refused to join for obvious reasons. They often quizzed me about why I did not become more active in the Party or consider standing as an MP.

I also renewed my acquaintance with Joe and Olive, although by that time they were academics and highly successful lecturers at the University of Leicester. One of my lasting memories of Harold was at his 50th birthday party, when our old group was reunited for the first time in many years. They still regarded me as 'the young boy' and the banter was apropos. Harold sadly died at the age of eighty-eight in 2002, followed a few years later by Joe and then Olive. I cannot assess what I owe to these three fine people, and in particular Harold. All took me under their wing as a young, lonely Jewish refugee boy. They encouraged me to acquire knowledge and values in life, a social conscience and a philosophy imbued with a love of humanity.

Going back to my studies, during the unexpectedly long summer vacation we received considerable lists for intensive reading. Some students took jobs and I decided to do likewise. I noticed that Aquascutum, the West End firm of couturiers, was advertising for a window dresser. I thought of myself as artistic and I also fulfilled the other adjectives listed in the advert, so I applied. In an unexpected twist of fate, who should appear to interview me but the Jewish corporal who had originally found Hitler's Will at our camp in Fallingbostel. He interviewed me but courteously told me the job required professional qualifications combined with appropriate work experience. Later in life I realised what a highly qualified position it was and was amazed at my audacity to even think of applying for this job. I chalked it up as a learning experience.

In 1948 the first Olympic Games were held since before the war. Although the Olympics had been hosted in London back in 1908, the Olympic Committee awarded the 1948 games to Great Britain. The journey from Stoke Newington to Wembley Stadium was not at all easy and sometimes entailed long waits for buses and the tube. But when young and impatient, all is bearable. I bought serial tickets for the athletic events at the reasonable price of £2 10s. The seat was well located, being about ten yards from the sprint starting line, kept the sun away from my face and gave me an excellent view. Fanny Blankers-Koen from Holland became a household name. Even she looked surprised at her success of winning four titles as a thirty-year-old married woman with two children. She most probably could have won more medals had she not been barred from several events by the then existing rules. The name Koen suggested that she may have been Jewish but, on being interviewed and asked this question, she said: 'I do not think so.'

At the end of September 1948 I was back at college, but with no thought of what to do when I finished. I was still in cloud cuckoo land, believing the world was my oyster. A fellow student and opera fan like myself obtained a list of forthcoming performances and I stood outside the Covent Garden Opera House queuing for amphitheatre tickets. Limited to six performances I spent a small fortune and walked off feeling a little lighter. If I remember correctly, the cost of the tickets was 4s. 6d. each and were the front seats on either side of the amphitheatre stalls. At times, owing to lack of money, we were forced to buy the cheapest seats in the house, i.e. in the balcony, which meant limited viewing. On increasing my income I graduated from the balcony with honours. Years later, my wife Shirley and I continued to buy wholesale tickets there, but we never abandoned our *stammplatz* seats, even when our children were old enough to join us. We continued opting for these seats as a matter of tradition.

A particularly funny episode happened during a performance of Wagner's *Valkure*. In the last Act, Hans Hotter was singing an aria in his inimitable bass/baritone voice, when the stage on which he stood, spear in hand and horned helmet on his head, appeared to slide slightly downward. At first it gave the impression of being either an optical illusion or a trick of the lights. The stage gradually gave way and you saw him very slowly sinking until he faded out of sight. But he had presence, and despite disappearing into oblivion he kept on singing and his sonorous forte voice could, nevertheless, still be heard. Immediately he finished his aria he received a roaring, sustained and unforgettable applause.

The last semester came. Those students who had no intention of taking their finals did not turn up for the week of examinations. How they had managed to receive a full grant for the complete study period was more than ingenious. As mentioned earlier they had used a fictitious living address to qualify for the maximum grant, and for the finals had produced a doctor's certificate. I met a refugee who was doing an accountancy course at Westminster College who had served in the infantry with the rank of captain during the war. This brave man had parachuted behind enemy lines and after many trials and tribulations was captured and put into a German POW camp. Miraculously, he survived. We sat our examinations at similar times and met again at the appointments office of the ministry of labour. The five days of exams I found strenuous and a completely new educational experience. After each session a frustrating inquest followed, really of little value as nothing could be changed anyway. I realised too late that in statistics I had used the metric system in one of the problems; a terrible and unforgivable force of habit. The German song from *Die Fledermaus* came to mind: *Glücklich ist, wer vergisst was nicht mehr zu aendern ist* (Lucky you are if you forget what cannot be changed).

Due to the long period of waiting for the exam results, we were told unofficially that we had passed. Four months later I received my diploma by post. This time the mail did not fail as it had when I neither received the time, date nor the location of the degree ceremony. The diploma was printed on small parchment with a list of the subjects passed printed on the back. It was quite unimpressive. As we say in German: *Glueck im unglueck* (luck in misfortune).

Sunday 1 January 1949 is indelibly imprinted in my mind and that of my family forever. With exams finished, it was time to celebrate. A New Year's Day dance was held at the Marcus Samuel Hall in Egerton Road, Stamford Hill. My close friend Mona and I turned up punctually, as was our custom, dressed in our glad rags with me sporting my usual bow tie. My friend prophesied that I would meet my future wife at this function. I was sceptical. But into the hall came a girl, quite out of the ordinary with very good looks. She appeared to be with a small circle of friends. I plucked up courage and asked her for a dance, followed by several more. We tripped the light fantastic and at the end of the evening she gave me her telephone number. We arranged to meet again the following Sunday.

The next week I called at Shirley's home in Stamford Hill, North London. We decided to venture by public transport to Kenwood House on the edge of Hampstead Heath in north-west London; a stately house surrounded by beautiful parklands and gardens. Although it was a cold, dull, wintry day I took a camera with me. We did not notice the weather but talked and walked so much that we ended up some miles away in the Lyons Corner House, Piccadilly in the West End. There I was introduced to the salad bowl and my first lesson on how to pile a salad plate to capacity. To this day Shirley's love of salads has not diminished and this is reflected in our blood pressure – hers is low and mine is high.

Then came a period of discovery for us both: Shirley played piano and sang and I played violin and sang. We had a strong musical connection. I had once been a chorister in the Alte Synagoge in Berlin, and she as a chorister with the School Choirs in the Albert Hall in London. We decided to combine our talents and started to meet at her home where she accompanied me on the piano. We sang duets from the operettas and musicals. We spent almost every day together. Fortunately I did not have to go home for my meals as Shirley's mother always made me feel welcome and invited me to have food with the family, which consisted of my future father-in-law and Shirley's two younger, giggling sisters Molly and Ruth.

Shirley and I became very close, but I still had to sort out my long-term employment which was not easy as a refugee. My ex-refugee friend from Westminster College who had finished his accountancy course was also looking for a job. He explained to me the difficulties he was encountering. We exchanged notes and came to the conclusion, rightly or wrongly, that it was because we were refugees from Germany that we were not being fitted up with the right job. The problems we seemed to experience were not the same for our fellow British students.

As it was not my wish to work on Saturday, i.e. the Jewish Sabbath, I registered for a job with the Sabbath Observance Bureau (a Jewish employment agency). They suggested an export firm by the name of Ensyda Ltd whose offices were in Oxford Street between Tottenham Court Road and Oxford Circus. Everything appealed to me, including the boss Mr Rosenbaum and the small business he ran. On the smallish side, grey haired and with a distinct East German accent, he had been engaged by Universal Plastics as their sole agent to develop their foreign trade. The future of the British manufacturing industry started to rely more and more on export, and plastic goods were in great demand. It expanded rapidly and replaced metal. Used in the production of toys it proved safer, cheaper and easier to make. Rosenbaum realised the potentials. I worked with this firm for about a year but, because this was a one-man band with a secretary, Mr Rosenbaum's business had limits as to what it could pay me, so we parted as friends.

Then I learned more and gained further experience about the export trade with several other firms, working for a time for a company exporting well-known brands of watches to Australia. I had a fine, roomy and comfortable office, was well paid and my prospects looked rosy. Until one day, the director stalked into my office looking for some missing documents; he picked up all the files and papers on my desk, threw them into the air, where they came raining down on my head. Aware that he was receiving regular psychiatric treatment, but not expecting such an explosion of fury and aggression, I picked up my hat and said goodbye.

Food parcels, to relieve the shortages in Britain, continued arriving from Australia for several months after I left the firm. Ironically, one arrived on Shirley's and my wedding day. On 11 February 1951, Shirley and I were married in Shackleton Road Synagogue, Stoke Newington.

The next export firm I worked for dealt with a miscellany of goods and was happily situated close to the Anglo-Palestine Bank (later Anglo-Israel Bank and now Bank Leumi), where Shirley worked for many years. We travelled to work together, met up for lunch and returned home together. I did exceedingly well in the export trade of cable wire where I caught the attention of the supplier. We had lunch together one day and he put a proposition to me: that we form a company together of equal partnership. My offices would be in his large building near Kings Cross and to start with I would engage a secretary to assist me. We agreed a reasonable gross rent for the premises.

He confirmed all these arrangements in writing and I gave notice at my existing employment. Suddenly, I had a telephone call from him saying it would be a good idea if ten per cent of the shares were held by a reputable firm of accountants. I had a dilemma. I no longer had a job and found it difficult to extricate myself. I believed in the honesty and integrity of the man and his sincere willingness to make the company a success. He had entertained Shirley and I at his home and exuded wealth – a Bentley and a Rolls Royce stood in the large driveway to his house. We were a very young newly-married couple and were flattered and impressed by his attentions. For the time being I did not engage a secretary but worked alone building up the business. It increased in line with my expectations. Then we agreed to employ a Secretary. He suggested he had the right person for me and arranged for her to start work. She turned out to be a very good friend of his. After a short while, I decided to employ someone else. However, the lady in question continued to visit the office regularly.

It was now 1953 and I had not seen my parents for nearly fifteen years. They and my brother were living in Israel. Shirley and I decided to make the trip to Israel to see them. It would be an emotional reunion. We set aside three weeks in June and made plans. We arranged to fly and I paid the enormous sum of £125 each, at that time equivalent to ten per cent deposit on a roomy semi-detached house with garage. Meanwhile people at the bank where Shirley worked advised her to purchase some shares which would double in value within a very short time. As we had no spare cash I passed this information on to my secretary, who decided to take up the offer and gave me £50 to invest.

The flight by Argonaut from London Heathrow took eleven hours, with a one-hour stop in Frankfurt and an hour's stop in Rome. During the last stage of the journey it was night and the lights were dimmed. Almost everyone on the plane was asleep except me. As was the custom in those days the captain came out from the cockpit and spoke to the passengers. He enquired why I was still awake and I explained to him that I had not seen my family since before the war. He thought my story exciting and moving and wished me well.

Arriving at Lud Airport and getting out of the plane, the heat and dust hit us immediately. More than twenty people were waiting there to welcome us. I was shocked when I saw my mother, whose black hair had turned snow white, and my slight father with his thinning hair. There were tears, hugs and kisses from my Uncle Pinkus, Aunt Erna and my cousins. The only missing person was my brother Saul (formerly Sigbert) who was in the army. We piled into taxis and made our way southwards through barren countryside for about forty miles to Rehovot where my parents lived. I was visibly shocked and upset to see their extremely primitive living conditions. Although I understood Rehovot was no Berlin and Israel no Germany, the contrast and hardship was still greater than I had expected.

Later that evening, mentally and physically exhausted, we fell asleep. Suddenly, during the night, Shirley sat bolt upright in bed and said: 'My Dad is calling me – something has happened.' I had to tell her that on the way to the airport my mother-in-law had confided in me that her father had had a heart attack the night before and was in hospital. They had decided that as he was stable Shirley should not be told and we should continue with our flight. Unable to sleep, we telephoned London the next day and were assured that he was recovering and in no danger.

As time went on, I still had not seen my brother because of his military service. My parents suggested that we go to the town major to ask for compassionate leave. The visit was scheduled for three o'clock. Being punctual I was first in the queue. After waiting for an hour we were told the major was delayed and would arrive at 5.30 instead. Returning on time I was once again first in the queue. After forty-five minutes we were informed again that he would be late and we should come back next morning. We learned fast. This time we were not at the front of the queue. But we did see the major and the appeal was successful. Some hours later my six-foot-tall, reddish-blonde-haired brother appeared, the brother I had not seen for fifteen years. We embraced and kissed.

Relaxed, Shirley and I continued with our holiday. My parents had no car and it was unbearably hot. The air was humid and there was dust everywhere, and wherever we wanted to go we had to walk to or take a bus. Public transport was an adventure and an experience. We could hear a host of different languages around us. People from all over Europe had a sense of expectation. Queues existed but not English style, and when the bus eventually arrived it was a free for all. Shirley had developed a heat allergy which caused her legs to swell and large blisters to appear. Fortunately we managed to find seats on the bus, but the passengers all seemed to be either a doctor or some medical specialist. On seeing the blisters they diagnosed her and suggested treatment; sometimes arguing and contradicting each other. Then a woman boarded carrying a large basket containing several live chickens, and being polite we made room for her. Gradually, with the bus heaving from side to side on the way up to Jerusalem, the woman occupied more room and I was eventually pushed from my seat. Travelling this way was certainly eventful.

Our first priority was to visit as many relatives and old friends as possible. We became accustomed to travelling in my uncle's Tnuva milk lorry, embracing, hugging and kissing relatives that I had not seen since I was a little boy in Berlin. We had a luxurious break. The bank which Shirley worked for made a car and driver available to us for several days to tour the country and take us wherever we wished to go. We drove through the Negev as far south as Eilat, which at that time had only one hotel and several unfinished buildings, and also Netanya, which was in its infancy with just one road and a few isolated houses. We then went as far north as Nahariya which had a very large number of German refugees. The story goes they were either doctors, lawyers or architects. We then travelled west to the Dead Sea.

Saying goodbye to my parents was not easy. The question I posed to myself was not easy. When would I or my parents have the money to meet again? Parting was very painful and tears were shed.

An unusual scenario confronted me when I returned to the office after the trip to Israel. Apparently my secretary, who had advanced £50 to take advantage of the share deal, thought that we had absconded with the money. She had approached my partner and even the Anglo-Palestine Bank. Meanwhile, the deal had gone through and she had doubled her money, but she also got the sack.

My turnover increased and business did well. I did all the work while my partner drew off his fifty per cent plus fleecing the company with increased overheads. It was time to say goodbye. I cut my losses and set up my own exporting firm in the City of London, on the second floor of an old Victorian building overlooking Liverpool Street Station. The first floor was occupied by a very charming retired naval commander.

He was an agent dealing in motor parts. He was married but with no children, only a lovely dog. We had a marvellous rapport. He was a Freemason of a Naval Lodge which included members of the Royal family. He wanted me to join his lodge but I preferred to devote my energy to making my business successful. Later in life, a number of my very good friends tried to persuade me to join the Masons, but I always seemed to have too many other interests.

I made a success of my export business and one day found myself at the British Industries Fair. Walking round I saw a large impressive stand of Scotch whisky trading under the name of Nicolson & Sons. I had received an enquiry from the United States about whisky, so I approached someone on the stand and asked whether they would be free to supply their brand to Chicago, Illinois. The answer was a quick and emphatic 'No'. I asked whether they would be interested in expanding their trade and they replied a clear 'Yes'. A middle-aged gentleman approached me and explained that they were a family business and owned more than 200 public houses in the Windsor area. The Government had made it manifestly apparent that the export trade was important and imperative for survival; and dollar earners in particular received support from the government. After explaining the potential of exporting, they invited me to come to their brewery near Windsor for lunch. During lunch we established a very good relationship and the manager spoke very proudly of being the father of five sons.

My contact in Chicago was a man by the name of Harold Frisch. A month or so before, he had given me to understand that he had a substantial number of outlets in the whole of Illinois and the surrounding areas for good-quality blended Scotch whisky, with the minimum age of four years. Nicolsons blend met these criteria and even contained whisky of seven to ten years. Certain areas in the United States had preference for either lighter or darker blends and one could blend the colour of the whisky in accordance with the importers' requirements.

Mr Frisch supplied his own labels and the first sample order went out and proved a success. Nicolsons had only a certain quantity available for export but Frisch was contracted to take the entire quota. It was a success.

I learned very quickly that shipping to North America produced climatic and geographical problems. For places in the Hudson Bay area one had to be aware that during the period of mid-October to mid-March, the sea, the rivers and the lakes froze. Whisky consignments had to go out before the first week in October, and Nicholsons and I had to be on our toes to see that these requirements were met. This caused major headaches. The whisky had to be ready, the bottling done on time and, above all, the labelling had to be perfect. Who would have thought that exporting to North America presented such difficulties?

Business was thriving and Shirley and I were able to buy a house. We were thrilled when Shirley became pregnant and our first baby was born in 1956. We had a lovely girl and called her Janice Aviva and she was, especially for me, and our whole family, a great joy.

But there's always a fly in the ointment. Nicholson had an enquiry which they referred to me. An approach had been made by someone wishing to expand export of whisky to the United States. I brought this matter to the attention of Frisch. This man had access to further supplies of whisky which Nicholson could not meet and he wanted to join forces with us. Frisch came to London and we were royally entertained at this person's home. The prospects looked most promising. A further business appointment was made to which the man in question did not turn up. I telephoned on several occasions but he was unavailable. We were all bemused. What did he really want? We came to the conclusion that his suppliers wanted to cut him out and he had used us as a lever – he was a con man. Another learning curve in life.

Several years later I had an urgent invitation to come to Bray. My good friend, the manager, informed me that Nicolson had received a very good offer from Charles Kinloch, a well-known brewery, for their holdings; but that after the completion there would be no change – I would still be retained as the sole agent for export to the United States. Meanwhile, my client Mr Frisch informed me that he and his wife would be taking a suite for six weeks at Claridges. I met him shortly after his arrival for a business meeting and he expressed the wish to meet Shirley and the baby. Our family was a hit with the Frischs and we established a long-standing friendship. We met them several times during their stay and I even drew up an itinerary of places of interest for them to visit.

Certain people in my life left a lasting imprint. Harold Frisch was one such person; a tall, imposing distinguished figure, immaculately dressed and well spoken. In spite of this I discovered that he suffered bouts of insecurity. This manifested itself when he told us of a number of anti-Semitic incidents he had experienced: On one occasion, after booking a suite of rooms at an exclusive hotel in California, the receptionist informed him on arrival that they were overbooked. They apologised. At a later date he found out that Jews were not welcome at this establishment; and this was not a unique happening. He quoted a number of very similar incidents. Amongst the higher, wealthy echelon of society in America Jews were unwelcome. But one must not forget that this was during the late 1950s.

After some years, Charles Kinloch was taken over by Courage, and that spelt the end of the whisky trade for me and the end of a chapter. Meanwhile, our family became complete with the birth of our son Jonathan David in 1959, who was the first boy to be born in Shirley's family for a generation. Tragically, Shirley's father Harry died before Jonathan was born and so he never saw the grandson he always wanted.

I kept my offices and my export company intact. For a short period my brother-in-law Bobby and I formed a manufacturing company for children's wear. Bobby was a very good salesman and we had initial success. However, the ethics and morality of some of the people I met in commercial life convinced me that I had to turn my back on the rat race. My mother-in-law Annie supported me in this conviction.

By chance I met the Revd Dr Isaac (Harry) Levy, whom I knew from my early days in the British forces. I met him on several occasions during my communal activities. At one such time he mentioned that the manager and secretary of a Jewish Trust Corporation would be resigning and going into private practice as a lawyer. A vacancy would arise and he asked whether I would be interested in the post. He briefly outlined what would be entailed. During my student days I had acquired some knowledge of commercial law, but other than that my experience was very limited. I asked him for three or four days to give it some thought. I went home and discussed it with both Shirley and my mother-in-law. The consensus of opinion was to go for it – provided the remuneration was adequate.

I met Harry Levy again and he introduced me to the executive director Mr Osterley, an elderly barrister. We immediately clicked and he explained what was involved in the job. He suggested that in due course I should enrol at the Guildford School of Law to take a correspondence course in probate, equity and succession. We agreed a salary and a starting date. Very tragically and to our great shock, on that same day my mother-in-law passed away. Osterley immediately told me to take as much time as I needed. That gave me confidence in the man and convinced me that the step I eventually took was the correct one.

The position heralded a completely new chapter in my life. My work was challenging and rewarding and the cause satisfying. I drew up many thousands of Wills, managed small and large estates and created charitable trusts for individuals and organisations. It was rewarding to know that I had helped needy, oppressed people to migrate to a welcoming new country, and helped them settle and start a new, respectable life. It had its comic, as well as sad and tragic, moments. There were fights and confrontations, some seemed unbearable at times, but I tried to maintain the principles which I had acquired in my early life. I met diverse people: some exceedingly rich, wealthy and famous; others had very much less but thought they had a lot. I spoke to large and small groups in Britain, Europe and America, as well as to schools and other places of learning. I helped many and extended useful advice, becoming lifelong friends with some of them. In 1973 I was appointed director/manager. It enriched me and I hope some of it rubbed off on my wife and family. For thirty-two years this was a major and useful part of my life and, even now, after many years of retirement, I am still winding up estates.

Throughout my life I always involved myself in voluntary communal work. Starting as early as 1943–4, when I became sports director of the Bar Kochba, I engaged in promoting a series of sporting events for Jewish youth. This was also the year I ran as Maccabi champion at the British Games at the White City aged eighteen. Unfortunately, I did not achieve my usual spot. After all, they were my seniors and international runners. My success was that my name appeared in the programme. Communal work was as important to me as it was to my father; perhaps having survived the Holocaust and the war with my parents and brother I felt I owed something back. I officiated at the synagogue for several decades. For twenty-five years I served on the education committee and was one of the initiators of kosher school meals providing for over 1,000 Jewish schoolchildren in the Redbridge and Ilford areas. I was also an executive of the Mizrachi (the religious Zionist movement), a governor of the King Solomon School in Redbridge, and was for a short while a member of both the World Jewish Congress and Board of Deputies of British Jews and B'nei Brith. A major part of my spare time was spent addressing schools and sixth-form colleges, both here and abroad, on subjects of the Holocaust and Zionist movements. Meanwhile, my wife took pleasure in running her own small antiques business, for a time with her friend Audrey Cass. We both enjoyed this as we were, and still are, avid collectors.

But despite happy family life following the war, my past experiences were still to come back and haunt me. In the late 1950s, in a cellar in Munich, a hoard of documents was discovered and the name of Perry Broad surprisingly appeared in the newspapers. Alarm bells rang but I temporarily filed the information. It was, however, to resurface some ten years later. I was about to cross paths with Perry Broad again.

9

Perry Broad and the Auschwitz Trial

In the early 1960s I heard on the radio and read in the newspapers of the arrest of twenty-two people accused of war crimes in Auschwitz. As I scanned the list I found Perry Broad's name amongst them. I remembered the fifty-six-page document, or diary, he had shown me years before in Munsterlager detailing the atrocities at Auschwitz, a copy of which I had among my own papers in my attic. I wrote to the War Office enclosing this copy and enquired whether there were any objections to submitting it to the judiciary in Frankfurt where the forthcoming trial was scheduled to be heard. About two or three weeks later I received a reply confirming that there were no objections as it had been declassified. So I put the diary forward. A swift response from the chief prosecutor arrived, stating that it had produced great interest. He enquired whether I would be prepared to appear in person at the court hearing and give evidence. I readily agreed, thinking back to the times I had spent with Broad in Munsterlager.

I arrived in Frankfurt a day or so earlier to allow time to prepare myself for the hearing. As I had not been to the city for quite some time, and in order to relax mentally and physically, I took a walk. During the evening meal my thoughts were preoccupied with seeing Perry Broad again after so many years. The last time we met was almost twenty years earlier and so many experiences must have changed both of us. The thought occurred to me: Are we now on opposing sides or am I assisting him? In other words, what effect would my appearance in court have on him and his immediate future? My previous association with him, if I can call it that, became an enigma. Did he take me in? Will tomorrow, or the days after, give me a true answer to my questions? I cannot say I slept well. During the night my thoughts became more entangled. Nothing changed my resolve to speak the truth as I saw it. Let the judges evaluate the true importance of the diary and my testimony in this jigsaw of evidence.

After breakfast on the day of the hearing, I took a taxi to the court. Due to the immense publicity surrounding the Frankfurt Auschwitz Trials, the city hall, with its large public gallery, had been converted into a makeshift courtroom. Long queues formed, despite the fact that it was the second year of the trial; the demand for seats was still enormous. Seven judges were in attendance. Room had to be found to seat them comfortably and they were accommodated on the extended stage. A session was already in progress when I arrived and I was asked to wait in a very large room adjoining the main hall. I sat in an uncomfortable chair and felt very depressed, simply because of the effort I had made to come to Frankfurt, leaving my young family behind, and then being seated in a cold, unfriendly and bare room. To make matters worse, a policeman passed through chaperoning a man into an adjoining room; he left the door wide open, dashed out to fetch him a glass of water and then disappeared. It seemed quite obvious that the man was one of the accused who, on feeling unwell, was left by himself to recover. It appeared to be an endless period of time before he was collected and taken back to the court.

Already annoyed by my treatment, I had a further wait before being finally needed in the courtroom. I was collected and directed into the converted assembly hall. I entered the hall and took my place on the raised dais. It became clear to me why this particular venue had been chosen. To the left were seated nearly all the defendants, together with their respective counsels and their advisers and assistants; and to the right sat the prosecuting counsel with their entourage. There were a great number of interested parties, as well as the worldwide press occupying the rear of the hall. In the gallery sat the public. The first one or two rows were reserved for VIPs. I was sworn in and the questioning began in German.

When I had finished my evidence, the chairman of the court interrupted the proceedings to welcome in the sixty-nine-year-old international Jewish leader and world chairman of the Zionist Federation,

Nahum Goldman, accompanied by his entourage. They took their seats in the front row of the public gallery. My father revered this man and to my family and me he was a legendary figure. Understandably, the judge paid him this honour. The chairman then continued and announced that the diary of Perry Broad would be read aloud to the court; the reading to be shared with two of his colleagues. There was a short break and then the judges reconvened.

After a short explanation about the background of Broad's diary, he commenced reading aloud to an absolutely silent court. The delivery of Perry Broad's diary made a completely unexpected impact amongst the public and officials in this makeshift courtroom. It impressed me greatly that the chief justice started the reading, two judges continued after him, and then he finished the last part. The descriptions read out produced diverse reactions from the audience. There were cries of horror and anguish. People screamed out and several fainted. I realised that when I had first read this report some eighteen years before, there was a multitude of horrors being continuously reported on the radio and in the press, and this report was just one of many hundreds. The atrocities had become almost part of daily life. I myself had visited Bergen-Belsen shortly after its liberation. Now, eighteen years later, when people thought they had heard everything and laid it to rest, it was suddenly all churned up again in greater force. Examined during the trial under oath, I confirmed that Perry Broad had written the diary by himself and that it roughly covered what Broad had told me in person.

On leaving the courtroom, a number of journalists waiting outside posed questions in English and German and took photographs. I gave a short interview for the radio and some television stations before returning to the hotel physically and mentally exhausted. Understandably, I could not sleep and reflected most of the night on what I had said or should have said. Is objectivity conceivable I asked myself? Did I portray prejudices in my answers? Had Perry Broad changed or was he still the same man I knew or possibly thought I knew? No clear thoughts were possible. I postponed my judgement and eventually fell asleep.

The next day, on my way to the airport, I continued to ponder my answers given in court. I had been brief, precise and unemotional, and assumed I had fulfilled all that was required of me. Before boarding my flight I hurriedly bought a number of German newspapers, putting them in my briefcase for reading on the plane. Again and again I thought back on everything which had taken place during the last few days. It all appeared unreal. The world I envisaged and felt comfortable with had momentarily collapsed. My pipedream world did not exist. Two decades ago people had fought to stay alive and saw their simple, innocent and hopeful dreams being shattered. Was this the true world I was living in or was it partly, or totally, hallucinatory?

On arrival at London Heathrow Airport I abruptly returned to the real world. There was the customary battle as people tried to leave the plane and then the unusually long queues before the luggage arrived. Yes, this is reality I said quietly to myself. I managed to buy a copy of the *Daily Express*. To my utter surprise there appeared on page two a report of my court appearance in Frankfurt. I bought several copies and proceeded to customs. To my astonishment the customs officer told me he knew all about me.

'Yes,' he said. 'I read the paper. Carry on the good work,' and waved me on. Fame at last, I thought.

During the homeward journey the world looked different. My attitudes and values changed. At home, my wife Shirley and our children welcomed me with love and affection. It struck me that seven days only had prevented me from facing a similar future to those in the Auschwitz camp, or from suffering the same fate as my best friend Siegfried Mandelkern, who was shot paradoxically after release from Sachsenhausen concentration camp. Returning to my family, I listened quietly to all the news during my short absence. Then I broke my silence by non-stop talking.

The following day at breakfast my children complained. My son did not like his Weetabix and had a conundrum about which cereal to choose instead.

'Cornflakes again,' my daughter grumbled.

These were momentary and real predicaments. But phases change in time, so I reasoned. Some childhood problems remain or become more acute in adolescence. They may either fade or disappear by adulthood. Some never leave until one reaches seniority. Nevertheless, to me, my children were and are a strong and permanent anchor. My wife and I gave them always durable love, shelter, safety, stability and security. All these irreplaceable assets totally deprived from those incarcerated victims of Nazism.

So I had given my evidence at the Frankfurt Auschwitz Trial and returned to normal family life, but I did not know the outcome for Perry Broad. Perry Broad's English name constituted an enigma and possibly made him politically unreliable. An intelligent, educated and cultured young man posted to the Nazis' top killing factory did not fit. Surely he could have been more useful to the German war machine in many other capacities? Those people normally posted to serve in concentration camps in a similar capacity generally had lower IQs and did not have his attributes. Did his father, his name, his early life in Brazil make him politically unreliable and hence influence the posting? True, his bad eyesight could certainly have been a contributory factor – he did wear thick glasses. From my experience he certainly did not conform to the archetypal brutal Nazi killer that was so often a guard or administrator of the murderous camps. What other evidence had been found and made available to the courts? Time would tell.

A year later the newspapers printed the outcome of the trial, with most of the background on Perry Broad's life coming from my own testimony: several generations back his father's family had come from Ireland. His mother was German and worked as a domestic in Rio de Janeiro. They married and he was born in 1921. The relationship between his parents became strained because his father travelled extensively and this led to the mother leaving her husband and returning to Germany with Perry, who was then five years old. She wanted the best education for him and he attended a Technische Hochschule and the Humboldt University in Berlin for several years.

When he was twenty, in 1941, he joined the Waffen SS as a foreign member. At the end of the war he was arrested in the British Zone. He cooperated with British Intelligence and was cleared and permitted to work in a clerical capacity and as an interpreter. He volunteered to write a report about his experiences in Auschwitz and was permitted to do so. Six copies were made on my instructions. (As mentioned previously, that is how I acquired a copy.) Twelve years later he was rearrested after the treasure trove find of documents in a Munich cellar but he was subsequently freed in 1960 after the payment of 50,000 DM as surety. He was rearrested to stand trial in Frankfurt am Main for war crimes. At the end of the trial in 1965 he was found guilty and sentenced to four years imprisonment.

Concluding my thoughts on Perry Broad, I continue to find him a very enigmatic and complex character. There is little doubt that he did not conform to the stereotype of concentration camp administrative staff or guards. Instead, he was clever, educated, cultured, talented in many ways, articulate and possessed of a certain charm. In contrast he displayed irrational hypersensitivity to any subject relating to the east. At the time I put this down to the then common German reaction, although perhaps not as pronounced or exposed. Subsequently, this all fell into place when he appeared in a number of major war crimes trials, for example, the Zyklon B Case Trial of Bruno Tesch, Dr Droshin and Karl Weinbacher in March 1946. At that trial he had appeared as a witness for the prosecution. At the Auschwitz Trial in 1964–5 he was a defendant.

The events of the war continued to surface throughout my life. Such a cataclysmic event in one's life cannot be erased or forgotten and I felt the urge to revisit the site of Bergen-Belsen concentration camp. Does a distressing and agonising experience remain permanently in your mind? Or does your mental defence mechanism store it away where it becomes less painful? The latter is, I believe, the case. The test came when I thought it imperative for my young family to see a small leftover or credible part of the Holocaust; hence our trip to Berlin, first to visit my parents who were living there temporarily. They were conducting a court case to receive compensation for the loss of machinery and other equipment during the war and contesting their pension. We stopped en route at Bergen-Belsen. I had last seen it in mid-summer 1945, now it was more than twenty years later. When we arrived the camp looked lifeless, but it still displayed the large monuments inscribed with the names of the dead, and nearby were the large mounds which were wholesale cemeteries. Gone were the ambulances, the barracks of survivors, the shrill voices, the endless visitors looking, searching, hoping to find their loved ones. Where were those who had miraculously escaped the fields of mass extermination? And those who had been buried in unmeasured, quickly prepared graves often unidentified and unrecognisable by their loved ones?

Bergen-Belsen is situated near the village of Bergen on the road to Hanover and not, as might be expected, in some far-off isolated place. Originally intended to hold Jews for the purpose of exchange with Germans in Allied territory, it later became a fully-fledged concentration camp, with the infamous Josef Kramer, who was previously in Auschwitz, becoming the third kommandant. In November 1945 he was tried for war crimes and sentenced to death. I remember repeating to my children the stories recounted to me by the Hungarian Jewish inmates, about how the camp staff were well fed but the inmates starved. A typhus outbreak killed tens of thousands of these inmates, including the young Anne Frank whose diary has become so famous.

The camp officially had room for 10,000 inmates. In actual fact it housed well in excess of 60,000, of which some 20,000 died in March 1945 and 37,000 died just before liberation. In April 1945 the British troops who liberated the camp were overwhelmed by the catastrophic numbers still dying on a daily basis. A number of Germans who worked as guards or in the administration of the camp feared arrest and prosecution, and they discarded their uniforms and dressed as inmates. Some were successful and were never seen again. Even when I arrived in midsummer 1945, ambulances were continuously leaving the barracks for hospitals with many survivors still not recovering. Twenty years later, the memories of that meal with the young Hungarian survivors continued to haunt me.

After the visit to Belsen, we continued our journey to Berlin where my parents were staying. After our arrival they listened in silence to their grandchildren's account of Belsen camp. The children seemed to be aware, even at that young age, not to ask Opa (grandfather) and Oma (grandmother) about their wartime experiences. An unwritten code prevailed. The wall of silence had penetrated even the next generation. At a very much later date I asked my children whether they remembered the trip. To my surprise they recalled very little, except for an incident with the porter of the block of flats where my parents lived: On arriving in Berlin we had parked our car in the courtyard and my parents had thrown down the keys to the rear metal gate entrance. As we entered, the porter came out of his flat and started to shout aggressively, saying in German: 'When opening and closing the gate you do it in silence. That is not the first time you've done it.'

I answered quietly: 'We are no longer in Nazi Germany.' I told him that if he had anything to say, he was not to shout, but speak quietly.

Not satisfied with my answer, he afterwards complained to my parents. Astonishingly, my father listened silently but did not reply. I was indeed surprised at his reaction but, on reflection, realised that his experiences during the war years had left him still traumatised. As time went on he became more and more withdrawn. My mother's reactions were not dissimilar but she confirmed to me that my father suffered severely from the Holocaust syndrome which included the fear of authority.

My daughter Janice's comments about the trip to Bergen-Belsen were this: 'I had more profound feelings about the Nazi caretaker of Opa and Oma's building. I was angry – this man still hated Jews after everything we had been through. How dare he? And how dare we put up with it.'

It appears that impersonal events are easily forgotten, but those which are personal are clearly remembered.

10

How my Family Survived

I had never really been told what had happened to my parents and brother in the intervening years between my departure from Berlin in 1939 and our reunion fifteen years later. As a family we just did not speak about it. As with many Holocaust survivors, there was a wall of silence. And our family was no exception. Then just a matter of weeks before I completed this book, I received a letter dated 24 January 2009 from my brother Saul in Jerusalem, explaining for the first time exactly what had happened to each of them during our separation. I cried uncontrollably when I realised just how much they had suffered. They had been separated from my father, with their chances of survival and escaping from Nazi Germany being incredibly slim. For them the dangers became worse after I left. My mother in particular suffered terribly. It all started with the arrest of my father. In his letter, Saul wrote of that day:

One morning, I think it was a Friday, two German policemen appeared at our door and ordered Papa to follow them to the police station. I think they told him to take a small suitcase. At the end of the day, Papa was back home and told us the following story, that Jews of Eastern nationality from aged 14 years upwards were rounded up and taken to a big yard where they went on identification parade. Father's police inspector friend, Herr Belgart, who the previous year had warned us about the imminent deportation of Jews and then the Kristallnacht, came to Papa's aid again. Belgart appeared, called Papa's name and two others, and shouted at them how he had told them before that they did not belong to this group and ordered them to return home. That's how he saved them. The next day, Papa was taken again by policemen and sent to the concentration camp Sachsenhausen. They sent him to barrack No. 40. Those who had arrived earlier were put in barracks 37–39. It is important to mention it, because from those barracks many Jews were brutally killed on arrival, or close to their day of arrival in the camp. Belgart explained afterwards that, unfortunately, he had left Papa's files on his desk. The next day his deputy discovered them and sent policemen to look for Papa.

While my father was in Sachsenhausen, mother had changed. According to Saul, all her hair turned grey over that year. She became very energetic and did not give up in her fight to get father released. She contacted all kinds of sources to get the maximum information on how to release him.

'In the meantime,' comments Saul, 'our radio and telephone were confiscated.'

One of the suggestions was to get a visa to a South American country like Uruguay or Paraguay, but the procedure was very expensive. My mother started to work; sometimes she took Saul with her. On other occasions he went with Uncle Arthur to collect money from borrowers who had refused to pay him back. One day, Saul was taken to a home for Jewish children where the unqualified staff were unable to work with so many different children. It was a terrible place and the children were forced to eat. Saul complained to my mother and he was not sent there anymore. Saul's story continues:

One day we went to the Polizei Presidium because Mama needed an important document. Policemen passing by were saluting us and it was a very strange feeling. On our way back, we walked along the second floor of the Polizei Presidium, overlooking a big yard, which most probably was used for parades. Suddenly we heard a group of men singing. It was a very sad melody. I wanted to wait and listen, but Mama pulled my hand, which was a hint to leave the building as soon as possible. Mama then told me that they were Communist prisoners. Some other day, Mama was very nervous (a very rare phenomenon). She had to go to the Gestapo to get an important paper. I think that she was afraid she would not return home. In the meantime, Mama was forced to host two families in our flat.

I do not know if it was because she needed the money or was ordered by the authorities to give shelter to families who had lost their homes. In the front room, first left to the entrance, lived a couple. I think they were some relatives. A couple with two teenage daughters, called Disenhaus, settled down in our big living room. One day, at noon, when Mama returned home and entered the kitchen, there was a row. The Disenhaus family refused to pay their rent and started to attack Mama. The girls took plates from the shelves and threw them towards Mama, but hit their own father. His throat started bleeding. I ran downstairs and called the porter for help. He reacted immediately, accompanied by his wife, told them off and warned them that next time he would call the police – since then they stopped speaking to us. It became a difficult situation living under the same roof because when they went to the bathroom, they had to cross our bedroom. And when we left the bedroom, we crossed their room.

After nearly six months of tremendous efforts, Mama succeeded in releasing Papa from Sachsenhausen concentration camp. We met a different person when he came out. He had lost over 20 kg of weight, he had a very sad look and he was afraid to speak, especially in front of me, about what happened in that horrible period. He also worried about the future. He had to go twice a day to report at the police station, and was committed to leave Germany within four weeks. I heard, though, that he and the other Jews had been tortured day and night. One night, the guards forced them to run barefoot over a path on broken glass, while the SS hit them with whips. One day, a Nazi stood in front of Papa and was prepared to hit him with a heavy stick. At the last moment he turned and hit someone who stood next to Papa, and the poor man dropped dead. He saw your school friends in the camp and thought how lucky you were to have been sent to England. In Weissensee cemetery there was a special area called 'Urnenfeld' dedicated to the dead Jews from Sachsenhausen. Just before Papa returned from Sachsenhausen, I started to go to school, in the Kaiserstrs. We had no copybooks, we used slate and chalk to write our homework. I went to school until the summer vacations about three months later.

I learned from Saul's letter that father left Germany for Bratislava about three weeks after he was released from Sachsenhausen. He became the leader of a group of refugees, who joined a group of Betar members, the revisionist Zionist organisation. He boarded a very old ship with a big wheel on one side (like a paddle steamer). This ship started to sail along the Danube, but got stranded in no-man's-land between Bulgaria and Romania.

Back in Berlin, a new challenge now faced my mother – how could she leave Germany as soon as possible? She had no income, and the demands on the Jews grew every day. It was not long before Herr Belgart, our police inspector friend, came to our family's aid again. The rest of the story is told by Saul in his letter and quoted here in full:

It got harder from day to day to get food, everything was rationed, and Jews got less than ordinary Germans. At the grocery store next door, there was a sign that said that Jews were forbidden to enter the place. The owner told Mama that the Nazis forced him to put on this sign, but she should send him a note and he would deliver our needs, he even added some food more than the rations allowed. At the 'Palestina Amt', they told Mama that they organise transport to Palestine, but children were not allowed to participate. She was desperate and told the story to Belgart who had promised Papa before he left that he would personally do everything, that we would be able to follow Papa at the first available occasion. Belgart himself went to the 'Palestina Amt'. His appearance frightened them, and the official promised to put us on the list. With departure secured, Belgart came and asked Mama if she needed anything for the journey. He took her to Steppke, a store at Bahnhof Boerse, where she bought some linen she needed. He spoke to her as if she was his wife. He even gave me a golden ring, to sell it if we should need money later on our trip. I think that was the last time we ever saw him.

We left Berlin at the end of August 1940, the order was to leave individually and not in groups, although all the organisation was coordinated with the Gestapo. I think that Eichmann was involved. The departure from Opa was not easy, we had to leave on Shabbat. It was the first time ever for me to travel on public transport on the Sabbath. It was afternoon, and Opa was in bed. We all cried, I waited in the corridor, which was full of uncle Arthur's bicycle spare parts. Opa told Mama that with us he would be ready to go to Palestine. We boarded the train to Vienna. Mama found an empty cabin, but at the first stop entered an SS officer, and took the seat opposite to us. He started talking to us, and asked me how old I was, if I went to school and asked the name of the school. I knew that if I said the name, he would have known that we were Jews, so I made myself shy and leaned over Mama. I knew that she would find a way to change the subject, which she did. Fortunately, he left the cabin after about two hours.

We stayed in a Jewish hostel for a while. After a week or more we were taken to the wharf of the Danube, where four tourist boats waited for us. We boarded the *Schoenbrunn* which was very crowded; people put their belongings on the seats. We had no place to sit until the staff of the boat were ordered to make room for us. There was a shortage of food, even of drinking water. On the boat was room for about 200 people, but we were about 800. On September 6, we left Vienna and the next evening we crossed under the bridge of Budapest. We saw the big city full of light. Since Hungary was a neutral country there was no blackout. Next morning we continued to Giurgiu, a Romanian harbour opposite Rus'chuk [Ruse] in Bulgaria. Here at the wharf, green dressed Romanian police were waiting for the Gestapo boat, which followed our boat from Vienna. The Gestapo man entered our boat, made an inspection and left shortly afterwards.

As we arrived, we saw a black ship with a strange big wheel on its side standing at the middle of the Danube, exactly where the border between Romania and Bulgaria runs, called also 'no-man's-land'. On its mast was a yellow flag which indicated that there was a plague on board. This was the *Pencho*. The small Jewish communities at Giurgiu and Rus'chuk tried to send some food but had to bribe the local authorities to do so. From that ship, we heard a man shouting: 'Wir haben hunger' [We need urgent help]. To our surprise, Mama and I discovered Papa among the people standing on deck. I will never forget this scene. The leaders of our transport, together with the Jewish communities, succeeded in bribing the Romanians to supply food and some of their essential needs. In the meantime, we continued to Tulcea and left the *Pencho*. In Tulcea, we saw the *Pencho* again as they passed very close to our boat. The people on board were standing and singing the 'Hatikva'. From our boats we could hear the people around us joining in the song. Always when I remember this moment, I cannot avoid the tears in my eyes. They continued to the Black Sea, crossed the Bosporus and the Dardanelles. When they entered the Mediterranean they got into many troubles. The old ship was not suitable for these conditions and ran aground. After efforts the ship was released but ran aground for the second time. They swam to a deserted island, prepared a 'rope' made of sheets, and pulled the ship, so they were able to take some belongings and the rest of their food. They made a big SOS using their belongings. After 13 days of suffering, being very short in food and especially in drinking water, Italian pilots spotted them. The next day a ship collected them and took them to the island of Rhodes where they disembarked.

The Italian governor of Rhodes admired Papa's skills, brought him leather to make a bag for his wife. In gratitude, he gave Papa a permit to leave the camp and go into the city. He even allowed him to make more bags, which were shown to the public in display cases. After a few months came an order from the Italian government to send the refugees to Italy. The governor offered Papa permission to stay on the island, but Papa said he wanted to continue with all the transport. It was a very clever decision because a few weeks later, the Germans took over the island of Rhodes and murdered all the Jews. The Italians took Papa and all the refugees to the camp of Ferramonti in southern Italy, where they stayed until the British Army freed the camp in late 1943. They got permission from the British authorities to go to Palestine via Cairo, and they arrived by train on 7 July. They were sent to the camp in Atlit, and finally freed on 14 July 1944, his 49th birthday. Papa was able to celebrate in Havazelet, near Rehovot in Palestine with his wife and his younger son.

Back to my part of the story, as I mentioned before, the four very crowded tourist boats continued to Tulcea where three bigger ships waited for us in the harbour. These were the *Atlantic, Pacific* and *Milos*. The four tourist boats were not suitable to enter the Black Sea and the Mediterranean. Mama and I embarked on the *Pacific*. The great majority of its passengers were on 'Hachshara' in Germany and belonged to the Zionist group Hehaluzt. The sleeping conditions were terrible, wooden shelves similar to those in stores. The space between the shelves was about 90 cm. On the shelves, space was very limited, about 50–60 cm or even less per person. Some new refugees came from several countries to join our ship, including people who had come directly from Buchenwald concentration camp. In Tulcea, we stayed a while and finally left for the Black Sea. We stopped in Varna, Bulgaria, passed the Bosporus and the Dardanelles into the Mediterranean. Life on the ship was not easy. There was always somebody on deck with a bucket and rope to supply seawater to wash your body. There was a severe food shortage, so we ate biscuits instead of bread. When they got rotten, the same biscuits were served roasted. On the last night, the sleeping shelves were burned in the oven. The management of the transport told us that we were short of fuel, but I imagine that the real reason was not to show the conditions we had endured during the journey.

At the beginning of November 1940, we arrived in Haifa. For the first time we received fresh food and expected to get off the ship shortly, but soon we discovered that the British government had decided to deport us to the island of Mauritius in the Indian Ocean. Although German bombers attacked London day and night, they had enough time to plan sending about 1,800 refugees on exile to a remote Island. In the meantime, they transferred us to a bigger ship, the *Patria*. This ship had been used to mobile British troops. Here we had better conditions, but soon they brought the refugees from other ships too, first from *Milos* which arrived a few days later, and started to bring also from the *Atlantic* which arrived later on. Again it started to be very overcrowded. The leaders of the Jewish Agency, together with the 'Hagana', decided to prevent the *Patria* from leaving Haifa harbour, so they smuggled a small bomb into the engine room which exploded in the morning of 25 November 1940, just when most of the passengers were on the rear deck for inspection. It took just a few minutes and the ship started turning aside. Some people jumped into the water, but logs and big screws fell off the ship and killed most of them. There was a panic; people did not know what to do. Mama and I ran into the middle deck which was off limit for the passengers, and as the ship tilted, we found ourselves secure from immediate drowning, but trapped alone in a long passage. I started shouting: 'Rettet ein Kind' [save a child]. Mama always told me, in case of drowning, the first action of the crew is to save children and women. The ship was now lying on one side. We walked on the wall of that passage, above us the sky, and unable to free ourselves. Suddenly one of the crew, of East Asian origin, heard my voice. Mama lifted me, and he took one of my hands. I was free, but he was not able to lift Mama. The gap was too big. He reached only to the tips of her fingers and she slipped back. He tried several times, gave up and wanted to go on. I held his foot and begged him to keep on trying. Mama jumped, tried to climb the wall, and the man finally succeeded at last to grip her hand, and lifted her up too. Then our saver vanished.

Now we were on one side of the ship. We crawled to reach the water and saw a big barge leaving the ship crowded with survivors. Dead bodies were floating in the sea, and Mama tried to direct me … to prevent me from seeing the bodies. A small boat, which used to supply drinking water, approached our ship. Mama lifted me and put me on the boat, and when she tried to climb up, people behind her held her foot and pulled her shoe off. Both of us were now safe. At the shore, British soldiers took us to a big warehouse and served us tea with milk and salami sandwiches, which Mama did not eat because it was not kosher. In the evening, the British soldiers took us to the camp of Atlit. We stayed there until June 1941. We were sent to a hostel in Haifa and free for the first time after such a long period. The Jewish authority's suggestion was that I should go to a home together with other children who survived, to learn Hebrew and put on some weight. Mama went to Rehovot, got a job in a sanatorium in Gedera, not very far from Rehovot, while Uncle Pinkas was in the British Army near Cairo. At the beginning I liked being with children in that home in Haifa, but soon they sent some of us to another place, and planned to send the rest to a Kibbutz. That was too much for me and I planned to run away. When I was with Mama in Haifa, we had visited Rachel and Samuel Rappaport. I remembered the location of Rachel's shop, so one morning I left the hostel and visited Rachel, trying to steal some money to cover the fare to Rehovot, so I could get back to Mama. Rachel discovered what I did, and I decided to run away. I spent the whole day in Haifa, and in the evening I went to a park. In the meantime, the management of the hostel discovered my absence and called the police. They searched for me until they found me and brought me back to the hostel. Two days later, I got permission to go to Rehovot to be with Mama. It was on the last week of July 1941.

I was deeply touched by my brother Saul's courage to finally put pen to paper and tell me the full details of my family's miraculous, but difficult, escape from Nazi Germany. One man was responsible for saving the whole of my family, including me – and that was Herr Belgart, the police inspector in Berlin. But for his moral courage we would not have survived the Holocaust. He risked his own life to save ours, not once, but on several occasions. In a sad twist of fate he did not survive the war. Herr Belgart died in one of the Allied bombing raids on Hamburg in 1943. I was, therefore, never able to thank him personally for what he did for us. I am eternally grateful to this 'righteous Gentile' to whose memory I have dedicated my autobiography.

The Holocaust had an even more devastating effect on the Polish side of my family. I had first visited my Polish relatives after my bar mitzvah in the summer of 1937. I had never been to Poland before. I have strong, vivid memories of that visit which opened up for me a whole new world and different way of life. In January of each year, when business was slack, my father would go alone for a period of four weeks to visit his parents and family in Poland. His hometown, Przmysl, was situated in the beautiful Carpathian Mountains.

On his return his cases were always loaded with delicacies only obtainable from that area: cheeses, wines and all sorts of goodies. Immediately after my bar mitzvah in mid-August, my father decided that my mother, brother and I should visit his family. None of us had been there before. The first part of our train journey was uneventful until we reached Breslau, not far from the Polish border. A large number of passengers left the train but we continued to the border town of Beuthen. There we crossed the border and changed trains. The scenery dramatically altered, as did the comfort in the train. We now sat in uncomfortable, very crowded and noisy compartments. People seemed to have an unlimited amount of baggage and the train appeared to stop at every station. At Krakow the train emptied, the countryside changed and a more suburban-style passenger entered. It seemed to be a good omen for our destination. Arriving at the imposing station in Przmysl we were greeted by a row of fiacres occupied by my father's family. The first fiacre with white horses was reserved for the three of us. We felt like royalty. We were overwhelmed by the welcome and friendliness of the family; there were so many aunts, uncles and cousins kissing us. For the first time I met my Polish grandparents. There were no communication problems between us because they spoke German and Yiddish. We soon discovered that the organiser of this magnificent welcome was my Uncle Lezer at whose house we stayed. He owned a fleet of fiacres as well as dealing in horses. My mother and brother had a room on the first floor and I stayed on the second floor, with a lovely view from my window. Without being given time to unpack our luggage we were all seated at the large dining-room table and served a lavish meal accompanied by a sweet red wine. I felt it was another bar mitzvah feast. Everyone was curious to see and talk to the visitors from Germany's capital, especially the wife and children of their brother.

The next morning after breakfast, a boy slightly smaller than me but of my age appeared. He introduced himself as Kobi. He said his father was a hairdresser and married to one of my father's cousins. He was to be my guide. He became my very good friend. He took me to his father's hairdressing shop and then on a short tour of the town. I discovered that Przmysl was a fortress town with a very long and rich history, and was the second oldest city in Poland after Krakow, dating back to the early ninth century. With a population in the 1930s of 63,000, almost two-thirds were Roman Catholics and nearly thirty per cent were Jewish, i.e. over 18,000. The rest were of other denominations. At one time, father telephoned and expressed concern because he had not heard from us. Mail from Poland to Germany seemed to have been deliberately delayed, but my mother assured him that she had frequently dispatched letters and postcards. Unwritten and unsaid was the suspicion that the Nazi regime was withholding, inspecting and delaying the post.

In a town square we stopped for ice-cream and I discovered the Polish name for it was *lodi*. For five groschi we had a magnificent cornet, and during my stay that was my daily treat. The River San ran through part of the town and whenever the sun shone we took a dip. One day, while playing with a group of boys, the game became too boisterous and I was held under the water. My screams were misinterpreted and they thought I was enjoying it. I thought I was drowning and could not breathe. Eventually, they released me; I spluttered and could breathe again, an experience which has stayed with me to this day.

My uncle had a non-Jewish friend and business associate who owned a hay-wain. He offered to take the three of us and other members of the family for a hay-ride and picnic around the countryside. Someone brought along an accordion and as we rode along there was a lot of laughter and singing. I learned several popular Polish songs and I can still remember the words even now. This was the first time I had had such an experience. After we expressed our delight, we were taken on several other excursions. The element of freedom and fresh air gave us town-dwellers from Nazi Germany a sense of euphoria not encountered before.

A not so elevating event, however, happened on a Saturday morning when coming out of Synagogue and going for a walk. Dressed in my best white suit with gold sailor buttons, and wearing my *Schuelermuetze* (velvet school cap) with two gold stars showing my grade, I thought I would be admired. But when greeted with taunts and shouts by other boys of 'Heil Hitler', I realised the impact the Nazi regime had had on its neighbours. This was the complete opposite to what the regime had portrayed at home. It could have been a regional response; but I felt it was more widespread in Poland. During football matches with Polish boys these incidents were repeated, but perhaps not with such strong force. Nevertheless, they meant it.

My grandfather lived at Kopernika 75, a bungalow situated close to the river. When I visited him, he explained to me that during heavy rainfall the river rose over its banks and this caused flooding which affected the house. Distinct water marks on the wallpaper could be seen. While playing dominoes with him on several occasions he enquired how I found life in Germany, in a regime which was openly anti-Semitic. The uncensored press in Poland warned, in no uncertain terms, of progressive anti-Jewish measures, but also drew attention to the wider aspirations of Herr Hitler. Neither my father's letters nor the occasional telephone calls to his family ever gave any indication of the real and true state of affairs we were living under in Germany.

Towards the latter part of our holiday Kobi took me on a tour of several old synagogues, of which the oldest dated 1594. It was a fascinating tour. The story goes that as Jews had been living on the Jewish Street of Przymsl for such a long period, King Zygmund August had compassion and allowed them to build a synagogue. He also granted them commercial and trading rights. The Temple Synagogue in Przmysl, although architecturally beautiful, was skipped over by Kobi because it was part of the Reform Movement rather than being Orthodox. Kobi then took me to his home and we climbed the stairs to the loft. He and his father kept homing pigeons on the roof of the house. He very proudly told me that when the pigeons were released, they flew as far as Sweden and then found their way home. His neighbouring Poles had a passion for pigeon pie and from time to time a number of pigeons failed to return.

I was sad when I had to return home to Berlin. I had had a wonderful time in Poland. My Uncle Lezer, who had opened his house to us and made us exceptionally welcome, unexpectedly shed tears. My father's youngest, most vivacious sister, who treated me like a younger brother, embraced and kissed us. Hugging and kissing did not stop. They did not want to let us go, as though they suspected forthcoming disaster. Once again, a convoy of fiacres took us back to the station. My mother, normally so controlled, cried when we started the journey home.

I never saw any of them again. On 1 September 1939, Hitler marched his troops over the border into Poland. Two days later, Britain honoured her threats that if Germany did not retreat a state of war would be declared. It was too late. There was no chance for Polish Jews to emigrate. The worst possible fate was about to befall them. The borders were soon closed, trapping them in a country where millions would be murdered in the death camps. My relatives were no exception. There was not a single word again from any of my Polish relatives and that included my grandparents. In spite of all attempts to find out what happened to them, we found no trace. They completely vanished. No one knows how, when or where they died. But survive they did not. They all perished in the Holocaust.

Postscript

Learning from History?

I was one of the lucky ones whose immediate family survived the Holocaust. We were a family torn apart by the Nazi regime, but were reunited in 1953. That we escaped separately from Nazi Germany and survived is surely a miracle. Among Holocaust survivors there is a strong sense of the need to remember the past lest it should be repeated. We are always on our guard. To use a cliché: some claim uniqueness, others have uniqueness thrust upon them. How this applies to my life only the reader may judge. This 'revolutionary' discovery came after admitting senior citizenship. Everyone's life is different. To some there was nothing spectacular in surviving the Hitler era and the Second World War, but how one survived was the difference between individuals. There is, in life, a common and an individual experience. One may even say common experiences are individually shared. Common shared experiences may evoke different individual reactions which lead to diverse lifestyles. I consider my life to have been extraordinary in a variety of ways, one period of which was my time in British Intelligence at the end of the Second World War. Who could have possibly thought that a fourteen-year-old boy coming to Britain on the Kindertransport, would within six years be amongst a small group of German-speaking refugees in the British Army translating parts of Hitler's Will? It seems somewhat incredible and part of history in the making. That I, who had lived in the shadow of the Hitler regime for six years, had lost my country and adopted a new one, would be involved so closely with something personal to Adolf Hitler. It is highly ironic that it was a handful of ex-German *Jewish* refugees who translated for the world the last Will and Testament of Adolf Hitler.

I was assigned solely, of course, to translate Goebbels' addendum to Hitler's Political Will; I was involved in the investigation into the death of Hitler; I interrogated high-ranking Nazis and came into close contact with Perry Broad. How did I feel about them? And how could I do such work? In a way, what a responsibility for such a young man, the significance of which was lost on me at the time. We had no time to think deeply about what we were doing. We just got on with the job; so much was compressed into such a short space of time. But it was important for me to show a higher level of legality in my treatment of the POWs, whatever their rank in the Nazi regime. They may have perpetrated the most horrendous crimes against humanity and the Jewish people, but they were innocent until proven guilty. I had to be above revenge and demonstrate the overwhelming need to be fair and humane in the search for justice.

I sometimes doubt whether we have learnt anything from the past, especially the genocide and attempted annihilation of two-thirds of Europe's Jews by Hitler and his henchmen. At a rally to commemorate the sixtieth anniversary of Kristallnacht, Herr Herzog said: 'This programme against the Jews was one of the most shameful moments of German History ... a slap in the face of humanity and civilisation.' Germany expresses diverse opinions about the Holocaust. Novelist Martin Walser has called on Germany to 'free itself from the shackles of guilt. Auschwitz should not be part of a routine threat, a way of intimidating ourselves into a certain pattern of behaviour, nor should it be a moral clamp, not even a form of duty.' Many Jews who grew up in Germany and were forced to flee Nazism, myself included, have not received any form of compensation for material loss or psychological sufferings. The Germans, through legal wrangling, have avoided restitution payments.

In the early 1990s my wife and I were on a business visit to Berlin. One evening, while dining at a crowded and well-known kosher restaurant in the centre of the city, frequented by a cosmopolitan crowd, we were approached by a young man. He said he had heard us speaking English and asked whether he could join us. During the meal he explained that the reason for his visit to Berlin was to arrange an exhibition of his father's paintings at the Reichstag. The opening was scheduled for the following Sunday afternoon and he invited us to attend. He explained that his father, Adolf Fraenkl, had been in Auschwitz in 1944 and had survived. Subsequently, he had lived in Vienna, New York and from 1966 in Germany, where he had died in 1983. After the war, he said his father had suffered from severe nightmares and as a catharsis he had started to paint, depicting the many horrors of the camp. As a result, an exhibition entitled *Vision aus dem Inferno* had been arranged, to which we had just been invited. Grateful for the offer, we thanked him, but regretted that we would be unable to attend as we were returning to London that same day. He therefore invited us to attend the morning press opening instead, which we accepted.

On our early arrival at the Reichstag the following Sunday we were greeted by the exhibition organiser. He explained that unfortunately they were experiencing difficulties in hanging the large number of paintings on the walls, as they were restricted in the use of nails. They were, therefore, trying to devise an alternative method. As luck would have it, most of the paintings were already in place. Walking round the exhibition I encountered a young volunteer in his early twenties. I asked him in German what his impression was of the horrific and distressing subject matter of the exhibits. In a casual, offhanded way, he replied: *Das ist alles historisch* (It's all history). I asked him to elaborate on his remark. He continued: 'My grandfather maintained that the Jews lived very ostentatiously, driving around in large cars, dressed in furs and jewellery and they had it coming to them.' I responded that even if this were true, was it a valid reason to exterminate them? I left him without waiting for his reply.

These comments haunted me, and I often pondered why this young man had come to help with the exhibition. Did he want to earn some money? Did he know the subject matter of the exhibition? What prompted him to blurt out these remarks? Was this a failure of German postwar education? Is anti-Semitism still so embedded in the German psyche that it will never be eradicated? I am still looking for a plausible explanation. After all that had happened to the Jews and other victims in the concentration camps, that a young German man could say such a thing at that exhibition causes one to pause and ask the question whether we ever learn from history. Probably not.

I would like to conclude by paraphrasing from Shakespeare's play *As You Like It*: the world is a stage and all men and women merely players.

I believe that this is how every human being goes through life. In child-hood one observes; the next stage is the learning process where one has a minor role, which then leads to major parts. Soon you may become a star with everything that entails, and eventually you direct and produce the play. During the last stage one retires and thinks back, but it is not as Shakespeare says: *sans teeth, sans eyes, sans taste, sans everything.* That is his opinion not mine. I would echo the words of Winston Churchill, when he delivered his speech at the Mansion House in November 1942 after the victory in Egypt. He said:

> This is not the end. It is not even the beginning of the end, but it is per-haps the end of the beginning.

Our children grew up, studied and are happily married – Janice to Jay Leberman, and Jonathan to Elizabeth Abrams. We are blessed with six grandchildren. My brother Saul married Miriam and they have three sons and many grandchildren. As the Talmud says: 'If you save one life, you save the world.'

Hitler's Political Will

First Part of the Political Testament.

More than 30 years have passed since I made my modest contribution as a volunteer in the First World War which was forced upon the Reich.
In these three decades, the love of, and loyalty to my people alone have guided me in all my thoughts, actions and life. They gave me the power to make the most difficult decisions which have ever confronted mortal man. I have spent all my time, my powers and my health in these three decades.

It is untrue that I or anybody else in Germany wanted war in 1939. It was wanted and provoked exclusively by those international states-men who were either of Jewish origin or worked for Jewish interests. I have made too many offers of limitation and control of armaments, which posterity will not for all time be able to disregard, for the respon-sibility for the outbreak of this war to be placed on me. Further, I have never wished that after the first appalling world war, there should be a second one against either England or America. Centuries will go by, but from the ruins of our towns and monuments, hatred of those ultimately responsible will always grow anew. They are the people whom we have to thank for all this: international Jewry and its helpers!

Three days before the outbreak of the German-Polish war, I suggested to the British Ambassador of Berlin a solution of the German-Polish question, similar to that in the case of the Saar under international con-trol. This offer, too, cannot be denied. It was only rejected because the ruling political clique in England wanted the war, partly for commercial reasons, partly because they were influenced by propaganda put out by international Jewry.

I also made it quite plain that if the peoples of Europe were again to be regarded merely as pawns in the game played by the international conspiracy of money and finance, then the Jews, the race which is the real guilty party in this murderous struggle, would be saddled with the responsibility for it. I also left no one in doubt that at this time not only would millions of children of the European Aryan races starve, not only would millions of grown men meet their death and not only would hundreds of thousands of women and children be burnt and bombed to death in the towns, but this time the real culprits would have to pay for their guilt, even though by more human means than war.

After six years' war, which in spite of all set-backs will one day go down to history as the most glorious and heroic manifestation of the struggle for existence of a nation, I cannot forsake the city which is the capital of the State. As our forces are too small to withstand the enemy attack on this place any longer, and our own resistance will be gradually worn down by men who are blind automata, I wish to share my fate with that which millions of others have also taken upon themselves by staying in this town. Further, I shall not fall into the hands of an enemy who requires a new spectacle, presented by the Jews, to divert their hysterical masses.

I have therefore decided to remain in Berlin and there to choose death voluntarily at that moment when I believe that the position of the Führer and Chancellor itself can no longer be maintained. I die with a joyful heart in my knowledge of the immeasurable deeds and achievements of our soldiers at the front, and our women at home, the achievements of our peasants and workers and of the contribution, unique in history, of our youth which bears my name.

That I express to them all the thanks which come from the bottom of my heart is as clear as my wish that they should therefore not give up the struggle under any circumstances, but carry it on wherever they may be against the enemies of the Fatherland, true to the principles of the great Clausewitz. From the sacrifice of our soldiers and from my own comradeship with them to death itself, the seed has been sown which will grow one day in the history of Germany to the glorious rebirth of the National Socialist movement and thereby to the establishment of a truly united nation.

Many brave men and women have decided to link their lives with mine to the last. I have asked and finally ordered them not to do this, but to continue to take part in the nation's struggle. I ask the commanders of the armies, of the navy and the air force to strengthen with all possible means the spirit of resistance of our soldiers in the national socialist belief, with special emphasis on the fact that I myself, as the founder and creator of this movement, prefer death to cowardly resignation or even to capitulation.

May it be in future a point of honour with German officers, as it already is in our navy, that the surrender of a district or town is out of the question, and that above everything else, the commanders must set a shining example of faithful devotion to duty until death.

Second Part of the Political Testament

Before my death, I expel the former Reichsmarschall Hermann Goering from the Party and withdraw from him all rights which were conferred on him by the decree of 29 Jun 41 and by my Reichstag speech of 1 Sept 39. In his place I appoint Admiral Doenitz as president of the Reich and Supreme Commander of the Wehrmacht.

Before my death I expel the former Reichsführer SS and Minister of the Interior Heinrich Himmler from the Party and from all his state offices. In his place I appoint Gauleiter Karl Hanke as Reichsführer SS and Chief of the German Police, and Gauleiter Paul Giesler as Minister of the Interior.

Apart altogether from their disloyalty to me, Goering and Himmler have brought irreparable shame on the country and the whole nation, by secretly negotiating with the enemy without my knowledge and against my will, and also by illegally attempting to seize control of the state.

In order to give the German people a government composed of honourable men who will fulfil the task of continuing the war with all means, as leader of the nation I appoint the following members of the new cabinet:

President:	Doenitz
Chancellor:	Dr. Goebbels
Party Minister:	Bormann
Foreign Minister:	Seyss-Inquart
Minister of the Interior:	Gauleiter Giesler
Minster of War:	Doenitz
Supreme Commander of the Army:	Schorner
Supreme Commander of the Navy:	Doenitz
Supreme Commander of the Luftwaffe:	Greim
Reichsführer SS & Chief of German Police:	Gauleiter Hanke
Industry:	Funk
Agriculture:	Backe
Justice:	Thierack
Culture:	Dr. Scheel
Propaganda:	Dr. Naumann
Finance:	Scherin-Crosic
Labour:	Dr. Hupfauer
Armaments:	Saur
Leader of the German Labour Front and Member of the Cabinet:	Reichsminister Dr Ley

Although a number of these men, such as Martin Bormann, Dr Goebbels, etc., as well as their wives, have come to me of their own free will, wishing under no circumstances to leave the Reich capital, but instead to fall with me here, I must nevertheless ask them to obey my request and in this case put the interests of the nation above their own feelings. They will stand as near to me through their work and their loyalty as comrades after death as I hope that my spirit will remain among them and always be with them. May they be severe but never unjust, may they above all never allow fear to influence their actions and may they place the honour of the nation above everything on earth. May they finally be conscious that our task, the establishment of a National Socialist state, represents the work of centuries to come and obliges each individual person always to serve the common interest before his own advantage. I ask all Germans, all National Socialists, men, women and all soldiers of the Wehrmacht to be loyal and obedient to the new government and its president until death.

Above all I enjoin the government of the nation and the people to uphold the racial laws to the limit and to resist mercilessly the poisoner of all nations, international Jewry.

Berlin 29 April 1945, 4.00 hrs
A. Hitler

Witnesses: Dr Joseph Goebbels, Wilhelm Burgdorf, Martin Bormann, Hans Krebs

Appendix II

Hitler's Personal Will

Although during the years of struggle I believed that I could not undertake the responsibility of marriage, now, before the end of my life, I have decided to take as my wife the woman who, after many years of true friendship, came to this town, already almost besieged, of her own free will, in order to share my fate. She will go to her death with me at her own wish, as my wife. This will compensate us for what we both lost through my work in the service of my people.

My possessions, in so far as they are worth anything, belong to the Party, or if this no longer exists, to the State. If the State too is destroyed, there is no need for further instructions on my part.

The paintings in the collections bought by me during the course of the years were never assembled for private purposes, but solely for the establishment of a picture gallery in my home town of Linz on the Danube.

It is my most heartfelt wish that this will should be duly executed.

As Executor, I appoint my most faithful Party comrade, Martin Bormann. He is given full legal authority to make all decisions. He is permitted to hand over to my relative everything which is of worth as a personal memento, or is necessary for maintaining their present standard of living, especially to my wife's mother and my faithful fellow-workers of both sexes who are well known to him. The chief of these are my former secretaries, Frau Winter, etc., who helped me for many years by their work. My wife and I choose to die in order to escape the shame of overthrow or capitulation. It is our wish for our bodies to be burnt immediately on the place where I have performed the greater part of my daily work during the course of my 12 years' service to my people.

Berlin, 29 April 45, 4.00 hrs
A. Hitler

Witnesses: Martin Bormann, Dr Goebbels, Nicolaus von Below

Appendix III

Goebbels' Addendum to Hitler's Will

Reichsminister Dr Goebbels – Appendix to the Führer's Political Testament

The Führer has ordered me to leave Berlin if the defence of the Reich capital collapses and take part as a leading member in a government appointed by him.

For the first time in my life I must categorically refuse to obey an order of the Führer. My wife and children join me in this refusal. Otherwise, apart from the fact that on grounds of fellow feeling and personal loyalty we could never bring ourselves to leave the Führer alone in his hour of greatest need, I would appear for the rest of my life as a dishonourable traitor and common scoundrel, who would lose his own self respect as well as the respect of his fellow-citizens, a respect I should need in any further service in the future shaping of the German Nation and German State.

In the delirium of treason which surrounds the Führer in these most critical days of the war, there must be at least some people to stay with him unconditionally until death, even if this contradicts the formal, and from a material point of view, entirely justifiable order which he gives in this political testament.

I believe that I am thereby doing the best service to the future of the German people. In the hard times to come, examples will be more important than men. Men will always be found to show the nation the way out of its tribulations, but a reconstruction of our national life would be impossible if it were not developed on the basis of clear and easily understandable examples.

For this reason, together with my wife, and on behalf of my children, who are too young to be able to speak for themselves, but who, if they were sufficiently old, would agree with this decision without reservation, I express my unalterable decision not to leave the Reich capital even if it falls and, at the side of the Führer to end a life which for us personally will have no further value if I cannot spend it in the service of the Führer and by his side.

Berlin 29 April 1945, 5.30 hrs
Signed: Dr Goebbels

Bibliography

Papers and Archives

The Imperial War Museum; the Association of Jewish Ex-service Men and Women (AJEX); the Association of Jewish Refugees; the Public Record Office, ref: WO 208/3779 (The Last Will and Testament of Adolf Hitler) and WO 208/3781 (Investigations into the last days and death of Adolf Hitler).

Newspaper reports of the Frankfurt Auschwitz Trial which mention Herman Rothman's evidence as a witness: the *Daily Express*, 21 April 1964, p. 2; *Jewish Chronicle*, 8 May 1964, p. 16; *New York Times*, 21 April 1964, p. 2; *New York Herald Tribune*, 21 April 1964, p. 3 and *Dienstag*, 21 April 1964, p. 13.

Books and Memoirs

Ambrose, Tom. *Hitler's Loss: What Britain and America gained from Europe's cultural exiles*, Peter Owen: 2001

Bentwich, Norman. *I Understand the Risks: The Story of the Refugees from Nazi Oppression who Fought in the British Forces in the World War*, Victor Gollancz: 1950

Berghahn, Marion. *Continental Britons: German-Jewish Refugees from Nazi Germany*, Berg Publishers: 1988

Cesarani, David & Bardgett, Suzanne. *Belsen 1945: New Historical Perspectives*, Vallentine Mitchell: 2006

Flanagan, Ben (ed.) with Joanne Reills & David Bloxham. *Remembering Belsen: Eyewitnesses Record the Liberation,* Vallentine Mitchell: 2006

Fry, Helen. *Freuds' War,* The History Press: 2009

———. *From Dachau to D-Day,* The History Press: 2009

———. *Churchill's German Army,* The History Press, paperback edition 2009

———. *Jews in North Devon during the Second World War,* Halsgrove: 2005

Gillman, Peter & Gillman, Leni. *Collar the Lot: How Britain Interned and Expelled its Wartime Refugees,* Quartet Books: 1980

Gottlieb, Amy Zahl. *Men of Vision: Anglo-Jewry's Aid to Victims of the Nazi Regime 1933–1945,* Weidenfeld & Nicolson: 1998

Grenville, Anthony. *Continental Britons: Jewish Refugees from Nazi Europe,* The Jewish Museum, London: 2002

Leighton-Langer, Peter. *X Steht für unbekannt: Deutsche und Österreicher in den Britischen Streitkräften im Zweiten Weltkrieg* (X Means Unknown: Germans and Austrians in the British Fighting Forces in the Second World War), Verlag, Berlin: 1999

———. *The King's Own Loyal Enemy Aliens,* Vallentine Mitchell: 2006

Levy, Isaac. *Witness to Evil – Bergen Belsen 1945,* privately published

Rossney, Harry. *Grey Dawns: Illustrated Poems about Life in Nazi Germany, Emigration, and Active Service in the British Army during the War,* The History Web Ltd: 2009

Trevor-Roper, Hugh. *The Last Days of Hitler,* Pan Books: 2002 edition.

Index

Lightning Source UK Ltd.
Milton Keynes UK
UKOW04f2335300614

234305UK00001B/12/P